MW00852523

Ain't Gonna Let Nobody Turn Me Around

AIN'T GONNA LET NOBODY TURN ME AROUND

STORIES OF CONTEMPLATION AND JUSTICE

EDITED BY
THERESE TAYLOR-STINSON

Church Publishing
NEW YORK

Copyright © 2017 by Therese Taylor-Stinson

All rights reserved. No part of this book may be reproduced, stored in a retrieval system, or transmitted in any form or by any means, electronic or mechanical, including photocopying, recording, or otherwise, without the written permission of the publisher.

Unless otherwise noted, the Scripture quotations contained herein are from the New Revised Standard Version Bible, copyright © 1989 by the Division of Christian Education of the National Council of Churches of Christ in the U.S.A. Used by permission. All rights reserved.

Scripture quotations marked (NIV) are taken from the Holy Bible, New International Version®, NIV®. Copyright © 1973, 1978, 1984, 2011 by Biblica, Inc.™ Used by permission of Zondervan. All rights reserved worldwide. www.zondervan.com. The "NIV" and "New International Version" are trademarks registered in the United States Patent and Trademark Office by Biblica, Inc.™

Scripture quotations marked (The Message) are taken from *THE MESSAGE*, copyright © 1993, 1994, 1995, 1996, 2000, 2001, 2002 by Eugene H. Peterson. Used by permission of NavPress. All rights reserved. Represented by Tyndale House Publishers, Inc.

Scripture quotations marked (NLT) are taken from the Holy Bible, New Living Translation, copyright © 1996, 2004, 2007, 2013, 2015 by Tyndale House Foundation. Used by permission of Tyndale House Publishers, Inc., Carol Stream, Illinois 60188. All rights reserved.

Church Publishing
19 East 34th Street
New York, NY 10016
www.churchpublishing.org

Cover design by Marc Whitaker, MTWdesign
Typeset by PerfecType, Nashville, Tennessee

Library of Congress Cataloging-in-Publication Data

Names: Taylor-Stinson, Therese, editor.
Title: Ain't gonna let nobody turn me around : stories of contemplation and
    justice / edited by Therese Taylor-Stinson.
Description: New York : Church Publishing, 2017. | Includes bibliographical
    references.
Identifiers: LCCN 2017017391 (print) | LCCN 2017036774 (ebook) | ISBN
    9780819233646 (ebook) | ISBN 9780819233639 (pbk.)
Subjects: LCSH: African Americans—Religion.
Classification: LCC BR563.N4 (ebook) | LCC BR563.N4 A453 2017 (print) | DDC
    253.5/308996073—dc23
LC record available at https://lccn.loc.gov/2017017391

Printed in the United States of America

Contents

FOREWORD: KEEP THE FIRE BURNING vii
Kirk Byron Jones

ACKNOWLEDGMENTS xi

INTRODUCTION xiii
Therese Taylor-Stinson

CHAPTER 1
Prayer and Social Justice 1
Ineda P. Adesanya

CHAPTER 2
Compassion 11
Therese Taylor-Stinson

CHAPTER 3
Home/Loss and Gains 15
Soyinka Rahim

CHAPTER 4
"Breathe on Me, Lord; I Can't Breathe" 27
Rosalie Norman-McNaney

CHAPTER 5
Love and Kenosis: Contemplative Foundations
of Social Justice 37
Gigi Ross

CHAPTER 6
"Pray for Yourself". 55
   Vikki Montgomery

CHAPTER 7
Howard Thurman: Contemplative and Social Activist 69
   Jacquelyn Smith-Crooks and Lerita Coleman Brown

CHAPTER 8
A Reflection on Contemplation and Social Justice
in a Global Era 85
   Jung Eun Sophia Park

CHAPTER 9
Religious Intolerance and Gender Inequality 97
   Ruqaiyah Nabe

CHAPTER 10
Multifaith Conversation as a Tool for
Spiritual Empowerment. 113
   Leslie Schotz

CHAPTER 11
Spend Time with Others: Prepare Your Heart
for Social Justice. 123
   Maisie Sparks

CHAPTER 12
A *Sankofa* Moment: Exploring a Genealogy of Justice 143
   Maurice J. Nutt

EPILOGUE
Contemplation in Action 159
   Therese Taylor-Stinson

ABOUT THE AUTHORS 165

Foreword: Keep the Fire Burning

While in the middle of preaching a sermon one night in my early thirties, I suddenly stopped. I had not planned for the sermon to come to such an abrupt ending; I was simply too tired to continue. My subsequent unscheduled journey through the valley of burnout led me to the writings of Howard Thurman. The words and witness of Howard Thurman (a name you will discover is mentioned more than a few times in this volume) not only saved my life, but transformed it.

Through his contemplative manifestation in deed and word, I learned that I was no less precious to God than the work I did or the people I served. I discovered that leisure was as much of a blessing as labor and that solitude could not only be as sweet as engagement but sweeter, and always, always had a way of sweetening the engagement that followed.

I found Thurman's blending of spiritually appreciative personhood with social awareness and activism to be compelling and, even more importantly, livable. Moreover, I have come to understand that cherishing personhood is an act of social benevolence. Only as we are our best changed and changing selves, may we offer our best changed and changing selves.

Thurman's wisdom-blend of personhood and service led to another convergence affirmed by countless contemplatives, many of them poets. I speak of daring to intentionally behold the splendor of life amid the scorching of life.

Somehow, along the way of my becoming a savior of the world, I missed seeing that the world was not only something worth saving, but something worth savoring. They who take the time to savor the world are in better shape to save the world. It is through savoring life, alongside our cherished sisters and brothers with which we share life, that we are filled with the just right inspirations and motivations to honor the relentless procession of life amid all that would threaten life.

To seek to save life without savoring life is not only risking exhaustion, but risking missing an abiding awareness of the Source of life. Sensing the Source is now my first and continuing deed of each new day. Sensing the Source allows us to taste wholeness and touch wellness when we are facing the complete opposite in our efforts for social change. Such tasting and touching is the stuff contemplative social activists are made of. They fight for an uncertain social flourishing from a certain personal fulfillment. They are continually—often strangely and surprisingly—refueled. The sources of such fulfillment and refueling are all around us. Whatever opens the mind and softens the heart has God's fingerprints all over it.

This holy book of wondrous story and testimony will feed you with some of the nourishing blendings I have mentioned above, and much more. Take your time; eat and drink these sumptuous offerings with head and heart; and dare to engage your social calling and endeavors from a place of deep and endless fulfillment—lest the fire go out.

Kirk Byron Jones,
author of *Calling Forth New Life: Becoming Your Freshest, Finest, and Fullest Self* and creator of "Yes to Grace" on Facebook

Acknowledgments

Writing and editing, to me, are fun, but it is also hard work, often involving long nights into morning. Yet even with all of the hard work I accomplish, there are lots of others who help to make a book possible.

First, I thank my Creator, who sustains me, protects me, and teaches me. I thank Nancy Bryan, VP for Editorial at Church Publishing Incorporated, for her kindness and patience, and all of the CPI staff who have been involved in the making of this book, its publishing, and the marketing effort that will take place to make it known.

I thank the board of directors of the Spiritual Directors of Color Network, Ltd., for their support and confidence in me to take on this particular project alone. Your blessing has sustained me.

I also thank all of the contributing authors in this volume for sharing your gifts with me, with our Network, and with the world, who will be influenced by your thought leadership.

I thank my Clearness Committee; my friend and mentor, Margaret Benefiel; and my dear husband, who encourages me and supports every idea I seek to fulfill.

Last, but not least, I thank Rev. Dr. Kirk Byron Jones, who so graciously, and without hesitation, agreed to write the foreword for this volume, and lends his name not just to this anthology, but to the membership of the Spiritual Directors of Color Network, Ltd.

Yes, writing and editing a book are hard work, but they are also fulfilling. And I release this work to you with gratitude.

In peace,

Therese Taylor-Stinson

Editor

Introduction

Therese Taylor-Stinson

Awareness Is a Hopeful Sign

Violence never really deals with the basic evil of the situation. Violence may murder the murderer, but it doesn't murder murder. Violence may murder the liar, but it doesn't murder lies; it doesn't establish truth. . . . Violence may go to the point of murdering the hater, but it doesn't murder hate. It may increase hate. It is always a descending spiral leading nowhere. This is the ultimate weakness of violence: It multiplies evil and violence in the universe. It doesn't solve any problems.

—Martin Luther King Jr.[1]

---

1. Martin Luther King Jr., "Where Do We Go from Here?," Annual Report Delivered at the 11th Convention of the Southern Christian Leadership Conference, Atlanta, Georgia, August 16, 1967.

As Dr. King reminds us, violence is not always physical, and the worst kinds of violence may be psychological. Racism is a form of violence that at times has been physical, but its most insidious expression is the unresolved trauma present in individuals and their families for generations. I believe this trauma has been, for centuries, unequally bestowed upon African Americans. I also believe that the years separating the legacy of slavery from its white descendants have left recent generations of whites with a cognitive dissonance that is also traumatizing.

On September 11, 2001, in New York City, terrorists flew two planes into the towers of the World Trade Center. The total number of people killed in those buildings and its surroundings were 2,606, as well as 125 more at the Pentagon in Washington, DC. Six thousand others were injured. Suddenly and unexpectedly, there was a new awareness in America that the devastation other nations have experienced—sometimes at the hand of our own country—was now possible on our own soil. The fear created on that heartbreaking day caused some to repress the truth of US culpability in the hatred some feel toward us. This "shadow," in psychological terminology, demonizes "the other" without accepting responsibility for our own actions or allowing compassion for the experiences of the other.

Carl Jung wrote, "Everyone carries a shadow, and the less it is embodied in the individual's conscious life, the blacker and denser it is."[2] One's shadow is not exclusively one's bad characteristics. It can also be denial of one's good characteristics—like the ability to

---

2. Carl Jung, "Psychology and Religion," *The Collected Works of C. G. Jung*, vol. 11, *Psychology and Religion: West and East*, ed. and trans. by Gerhard Adler and R. F. C. Hall (Princeton, NJ: Princeton University Press, 1975), 131.

love or forgive. Whatever characteristics we deny in ourselves, we project on "the other." The other can become victim to our negative projections or our admiration.

The shooting of unarmed black men by law enforcement officers and lone vigilantes ambushing churches has exposed the lie of a "post-racial" America. The polarization, violence, and controversies make it seem like there is no turning from our human condition. But there is hope: in this divisive time, we can provide safe spaces for all races and ethnicities to heal from centuries of white supremacy and devaluing the lives of others. It will require less focus on rhetoric and more on creative ways to build relationships across racial lines. It will require a racial awareness that exposes the lie and causes those of good will to examine their souls, seeing racism as a spiritual issue that begins the process of change.

Racism is certainly part of the American shadow, suppressed and repressed from our consciousness through structural and systemic means for over four hundred years, but that shadow is cast globally among all people of color. It is a violent shadow that aligns with America's overall violent history evident in the militarization toward black communities on its own soil. Statistics show that overall violence in America has declined; however, we are more violent than other affluent countries, and incidents of mass violence in the United States have increased. Our awareness of violence has increased, and we are more fearful. However, awareness of violence may be a hopeful sign, as we make more conscious decisions about its existence.

Only greater awareness and the spiritual growth that comes with that awareness can overcome the shadow behavior. With the murder of our sons and daughters and higher rates of incarceration, our family life is disrupted for generations. We are aware of these trends, attempting to mitigate the damage and even escape from the environment ourselves through education, assimilation, and surrender to the dominant culture. But assimilation is painful and difficult, separating us from our own culture and identity.

It may take time to awaken to the violence of racism imbedded deeply in our structures and systems. We are not aware of the many ways racism manifests in our culture and society. It may take a while to break a bad habit. Awareness is a hopeful sign we're headed in the right direction. Awareness brings us to making conscious choices about how we behave.

We must move toward awaking to the shadow of racism and becoming more mindful about how we behave toward "the other."

Contemplation and Justice

We are both connected and separate. We dwell in both, but we are not meant to stay in either. Separateness allows us to become aware and deepen; then, we are called to remain in that deepened place as we enter the connectedness of the universe.

The dilemma is to know when to remain separate and aware of oneself and when to integrate that more deepened self with the flow and connectedness of the universe.

I think about how the truth of the words I wrote above at a Spiritual Directors International Educational Event on April 16,

2015, in Louisville, Kentucky, lives in the Spiritual Directors of Color Network. In some ways, our Network has separated from the larger group of contemplatives in order to share our common experience more deeply and arise more awakened and aware of who we are and what our contributions to the larger contemplative community are. Then, in that more deepened and awakened state, we are called into the Oneness of the Universe.

We hope that the essays you will read in this anthology from spiritual directors of color will pull you aside to more fully consider these themes of "contemplation and justice." Though we are people across the African diaspora, as well as Asian and Semite, you will also witness the diversity of our group in our approaches, writing styles, experiences, thoughts, cultures, faith traditions, and passions around this theme.

At an annual Gerald May Seminar, hosted by the Shalem Institute, Jack Finley, psychologist, author, mystic, and former monk, defined contemplation as paying attention, "to reflect on one's awareness of the present moment." He said that "the mystic is known by the quality of their empathy, integrity, by the authenticity of your presence with each. . . . You cannot express the beauty of yourself and hide at the same time."[3] With that in mind, the members of the Spiritual Directors of Color Network attempt to apply a balm on the trauma of racism and other acts of injustice; to separate ourselves from spiritual disease, which would render us powerless; to awaken our senses to issues of justice, so that perhaps

---

3. James Finley, "Turning to Thomas Merton as Our Guide in Contemplative Living," Shalem Institute's Tenth Annual Gerald May Seminar, Friday Lecture, April 24, 2015.

one day we can enter into God's dream of Oneness that manifests itself in diverse forms to sustain the life of the whole.

We are not hiding. We are grieved but hopeful. We want to express the beauty of ourselves in ways that are healing. We are attempting to do the work that is necessary to be true to our calling as spiritual directors—to listen, to ask questions, to pray deeply, and to be an instrument for healing, for change, and for true unity with all its diversity in our broken world.

1

Prayer and Social Justice

INEDA P. ADESANYA

I come to the garden alone, while the dew is still on the roses,
and the voice I hear falling on my ear the Son of God discloses.

And he walks with me and he talks with me and he tells me I am
*   his own,*
and the joy we share as we tarry there none other has ever known.

He speaks and the sound of his voice is so sweet the birds hush
*   their singing,*
and the melody that he gave to me within my heart is ringing.
                        —"In the Garden" by Charles A. Miles

Isn't that a beautiful song?
     I serve annually as extended staff at a contemplative retreat. Known to be an extemporaneous singer, I was asked one year to sing a song, any song, and the song the Spirit put on my heart was "In the Garden." Many expressed gratitude that I had selected this song to sing because it had been "their mother's or grandmother's favorite song." They also shared how much they missed this song that had been banished from their churches.

1

You see, a few decades ago, many pastors and religious leaders began to reject this song because of its focus on the self vs. the other or community. It has been said that songs like "In the Garden" are shallow and thus produced shallow people incapable of facing the challenges of the world . . . incapable of doing the just work of Jesus Christ. It is my hope that you will embrace "the garden" not only as a prerequisite to doing justice and the work of Christ, but also as a tool for spiritual growth and sustainability.

My understanding of God's demand for justice, the importance of authentic prayer and contemplation, and the significance of listening to God is largely rooted in the Hebrew Bible book of Zechariah.

> Then the word of the LORD Almighty came to me: "Ask all the people of the land and the priests, 'When you fasted and mourned in the fifth and seventh months for the past seventy years, was it really for me that you fasted? And when you were eating and drinking, were you not just feasting for yourselves? Are these not the words the LORD proclaimed through the earlier prophets when Jerusalem and its surrounding towns were at rest and prosperous, and the Negev and the western foothills were settled?'"
>
> And the word of the LORD came again to Zechariah: "This is what the LORD Almighty says: 'Administer true justice; show mercy and compassion to one another. Do not oppress the widow or the fatherless, the foreigner or the poor. Do not plot evil against each other.'
>
> "But they refused to pay attention; stubbornly they turned their backs and covered their ears. They made their

hearts as hard as flint and would not listen to the law or to the words that the LORD Almighty had sent by his Spirit through the earlier prophets. So the LORD Almighty was very angry.

"When I called, they did not listen; so when they called, I would not listen, says the LORD Almighty." (Zech. 7:4–13, NIV)

Zechariah had a message for his people—and it wasn't a pleasant one. He needed the people to understand that simply keeping the rituals of the faith was of no value. It meant nothing to God because it meant nothing to the people. It was not helping anyone. They weren't doing these acts out of love and devotion for God.[1]

As a spiritual director, I am frequently asked, "How can I know for sure that I am doing God's will?" One way to test whether you are doing God's will is to ask yourself if anyone (any of God's creation) other than yourself (your company, your people, etc.) is benefitting from the act or work. Remember that we are to make disciples of ALL nations, love our neighbor, and show mercy and compassion to everyone.

One of my mentors in the ministry, the Rev. Dr. Kirk Byron Jones, frequently writes and speaks of being still in knowing that God is. He says that spiritual stillness is often unintentionally blocked by religious practices that can obstruct as much as they can enhance prayer, experienced as mere monologue toward God,

---

1. Stormie O'Martian, "Developing a Heart for Worship" Commentary, in *The Power of a Praying Woman Bible* (Eugene, OR: Harvest House Publishers, 2006), 1157.

which can be a form of avoiding God. We often end up talking ourselves out of God's presence. "We can also dodge God under the guise of devotion by reading and singing, without leaving openings for stillness and silence. We may go from song to song, and Scripture to Scripture, without ever taking time to absorb, to sit, to wait, to question, or even to doubt."[2] It is not enough that we should read about prayer, hear and sing worship songs, or listen to other people pray and worship. We must pray authentically, contemplate God's response and worship God with a heart full of love. It is in personal prayer times that an intimate relationship with God develops. Prayer is multifaceted. The intent of authentic deep prayer is not only to communicate, be in relationship with, and experience God but, moreover, to effect transformation in our lives and in the lives of others.

Being still before the Lord in contemplation is a form of prayer; worship is a form of prayer; singing can be a form of prayer; prayer can be communal or corporate; it can consist of petition or intercession; or prayer can be entering the garden alone to walk and talk with Jesus. Yes, there are many different ways to pray.

International prayer warrior Stormie O'Martian says, "If you are ever worshipping God by yourself and you don't sense His intimate presence, continue to praise and worship Him until you do."[3] By praise and worship, I mean giving God credit where credit is due. Rather than simply exclaiming that you praise God, tell the

---

2. Kirk Byron Jones, *Rest in the Storm: Self-Care Strategies for Clergy and Other Caregivers* (Valley Forge, PA: Judson Press, 2001), 84.
3. This statement is supported by information contained in the PBS documentary titled *2015: A Year in Mass Shootings* found at www.pbs.org/video/2365635992.

world the ways in which he has guided you and provided for you, the way she has protected and sheltered you. It's not that you have to try hard to get God to be close to you. He has chosen to dwell in the midst of your praise. But you do have to give her time to break down the barriers within *your soul* and penetrate the walls of *your heart* so that he can pour himself into you.

Scripture documents that a time of silence and contemplation was part of Jesus's regular routine, a method of spiritual care. After stories of Jesus ministering to crowds and healing people, Luke 5:16 tells us that Jesus often withdrew to lonely places and prayed. In the following chapter, Luke 6:12, just prior to selecting the twelve apostles, the Gospel tells us that Jesus went out to a mountainside and spent the night praying to God. Later in chapter nine, Luke tells us that Jesus prayed in private even when his disciples were with him and that he took Peter, John, and James with him up onto a mountain to pray. It was on this occasion that the three disciples would see Jesus in his full glory. Prayer is a time to experience wholeness from the inside out, a time to receive the love, grace, and peace that we then offer to others to God's glory.

Similarly, in the Gospel according to Mark, we understand that very early in the morning, while it was still dark, Jesus got up, left the house, and went off to a solitary place where he prayed (1:35). He did this just prior to expanding his ministry to go and preach in nearby villages. The Bible also tells us that after Jesus fed the five thousand and sent his disciples ahead of him to Bethsaida, he dismissed the crowd and went up on a mountainside by himself to pray (Mark 6:46).

These examples don't tell us expressly how Jesus prayed. I wonder if it was extemporaneous and kataphatic, or silent, centering, apophatic prayer. Maybe he audibly and/or physically praised God through song and adoration, or maybe it was contemplative and reflective prayer. What we do know is that Jesus regularly took time apart from his ministry for renewal and centering, for discernment and preparation.

In speaking on the history of contemplative traditions, scholar and theologian Barbara A. Holmes explains that "in Eurocentric contexts contemplation and silence were presumed to be synonymous. Unfortunately, the pervasiveness of this presumption helps to shroud the emergence of contemplative practices within the vibrant and ecstatic Africana traditions."[4] To be clear, in my faith tradition, intentional acts of contemplation must not always be silent or still, but can also be embodied in dance, song, and shout! A contemplative act is an act of deliberate consideration with the intent of seeing or experiencing God. Whatever act, gesture, thought, song, or word that reflects or brings us into the tangible presence of the Holy Spirit is an act of contemplation. For instance:

- In my faith tradition, we sometimes have devotions or begin a sermon with a "call and response" in the form of a long-metered hymn. In the deep, extended moans of the long-metered hymn there rests a space for contemplation.
- There is a faithful member of my home congregation who regularly but gently and ever so intentionally stands and lifts

4. Barbara Holmes, *Joy Unspeakable: Contemplative Practices of the Black Church* (Minneapolis: Fortress Press, 2004), 42.

his hands into the air pumping them up and down at seemingly random times during the worship service and sermons. I submit that this is an act of contemplation.

- Jesus's journeys into the mountain to pray were acts of contemplation.

- When Jesus hushed the elements, saying "Peace, be still"—that was an act of contemplation.

- When Mahalia Jackson proclaims, "There Is a Balm in Gilead"—that's a contemplative act. I, too, have sung this soul-stirring hymn and to do so authentically requires nothing less than deliberate consideration with the intent of seeing or experiencing God.

- Dr. Martin Luther King Jr. and thousands of others marched nonviolently for freedom and civil rights; when we march today to combat violence, hate, terrorism, oppression, human trafficking, and other injustices in the world, we are most often performing acts born out of contemplation, acts seeking holy presence and intervention.

- I've been told that my style of preaching presents as a contemplative act. My hope is that each time I stand before a congregation, through the words that I speak, both preacher and congregation, together, will see and experience God.

Although he was fully God, Jesus was also fully human. In order for Jesus to have the strength to minister continually, he had to make prayer and contemplation a priority. When painful things happened, Jesus handled them by spending time alone with God.

For instance, when Jesus heard about the death of John the Baptist, he withdrew by boat privately to a solitary place (Matt. 14:13).

There are numerous matters of concern in our society. Gangs and drugs continue to plague our urban areas and inner cities, only to be overshadowed by hundreds of targeted mass killings each year throughout the country.[5] Wars with other nations are a constant threat. There is a prevalence of both foreign and domestic terror, hate, and evil. We pray and cry out to God and observe all the outward rituals of religion, but we don't place a high priority in our lives on justice and compassion for our neighbor. It is important for us to not only be still, go into the garden, and cry out to God, but also to do what God says. To do that, we must listen to his Word and hear his call. We do this through prayer and contemplation. Matters of social justice must not be separate from our prayer lives.

I am a practical theologian. This means that I want to see theology in practice, in action! It is one thing to talk about good news, and another to *be* and *do* good news. This is reflective of my conviction that spirituality and justice go hand-in-hand. During the course of my ministerial internship at the Allen Temple Baptist Church (ATBC), one of our pastoral leaders, noticing my focus on Christian Spirituality, asked of my spiritual motivation for helping ATBC to challenge the institutional injustice of the Alameda County (AC) Transit's Bus Rapid Transit (BRT) proposal for East Oakland. I responded that my spiritual motivation lies in the understanding that spirituality and justice cannot be separated. There is no such thing as private spirituality. So it was quite natural that

_____

5. See www.pbs.org using data from Shootingtracker.com.

8

I was spiritually motivated to help prevent the impending institutional injustice threatened by the proposed BRT project. God gifts each of us with our own set of unique skills and abilities so that God can use us in the manifestation of his will in this world. God's will is gleaned most clearly in his greatest command: to love God and to love your neighbor. First John 3:16 explains how to know what love is: "[Jesus Christ] laid down his life for us—and we ought to lay down our lives for one another." Jesus tells us in the Gospel of Luke who our neighbor is in the parable of the Good Samaritan along the Jericho Road. Jesus affirms that the one who showed mercy to the contaminated, *marginalized, disinherited* stranger was indeed the neighbour, and that we must go and do likewise. When God shows us mercy, God does so in spite of ourselves, our situations, and even our sins. The Christian must intentionally put him- or herself out so that the wounds of the broken [*or would-be broken*] might be healed.[6] So my call to help others to experience spiritual freedom is likewise a call to help others experience justice.

After we go into the garden, walk and talk and *listen* with Jesus, we must go out and be the legs, arms, hands, and feet of Christ who lives in us; we must lift our voices for righteousness and justice. In authentic prayer and contemplation, you will sense your call, why you were created. You will hear God speak to your heart because he has softened it and made it less resistant. In deep authentic prayer, you will experience God's love. He will change your emotions, attitudes, and patterns of thought. God will pour out her

---

6. J. Alfred Smith Sr. and Harry Louis Williams II, *On the Jericho Road: A Memoir of Racial Justice, Social Action and Prophetic Ministry* (Downers Grove, IL: InterVarsity Press, 2004), 21.

Spirit upon you and make your heart open to receive all she has for you. He will give you clarity of mind so you can better understand his Word, enabling you to administer true justice as called for in the Zechariah text. I contend that God can and will refresh, renew, enrich, enlighten, heal, free, and fulfill you. The Holy Spirit will breathe life into the dead areas of your existence and infuse you with her power and joy.

The Lord, Jesus Christ, will redeem and transform you and your situation. This is what the resurrection was all about! He will fill your empty places, liberate you from bondage, take away your fear and doubt, grow your faith, and give you peace! God will break the chains that imprison you and restore you to wholeness. He will lift you above your circumstances and limitations, and motivate you to show mercy and compassion and to help others find life and justice in Christ.

As a spiritual director, I witness all too often Christians who are too beat and too busy to be the arms and legs of Christ. My theology of ministry seeks to assist Christians and others to lift themselves up through knowledge, encouragement, and spiritual guidance. The means and intended outcome are to more effectively communicate the ideals of the Christian faith, helping others to mature in their Christian walks and to become more confident disciples, spiritually healthy, able, and willing to follow Christ in providing and advocating for those who are poor, oppressed, and marginalized.

2

Compassion

THERESE TAYLOR-STINSON

Justice is what love looks like in public,
just like tenderness is what love feels like in private.
—Cornell West, Howard University Andrew
Rankin Chapel Worship, April 2011

My husband and I took a couple of hours on a Sunday afternoon to serve the homeless, to give back because both of us know "but for the grace of God, go I." A man walked to the threshold of the door, and I looked up just in time to catch his figure before he darted back behind a curtained window next to the door. He slipped his hand around the corner to grab one of the brown bags prepared for each visitor to take with them after eating the hot Sunday lunch lovingly served by members of the church. One of the church members saw him and invited him in for a hot meal, but he had seen me, and said he couldn't stay; he had a run to make uptown. I said his name under my breath—my childhood friend, from one of the families in our neighborhood. They were three brothers from interracial parents—handsome boys—and all three, including, I believe, their mother and father, sometimes rode bikes daily.

While working downtown, I would often run into him and his younger brother, still riding bikes, but now to make a living as messengers throughout the interconnection of businesses and government covering Washington, DC; Maryland; and Virginia. We would speak, catch up a bit on our lives, and then go our separate ways. Now I was seeing him enter a kitchen serving the homeless for something to eat on a Sunday afternoon. I wanted to speak out, "It's okay! Come in and eat!" I didn't. I stood silently and watched, wanting to hide myself, allowing him to preserve his dignity without even fully forming the intent.

I have pondered compassion for years, studying the etymology of the word, reflecting on how that word came alongside my own life. I have always considered myself an empath of sorts, and our culture has made the words "empathy" and "compassion" synonymous in many ways. I don't see these two words as synonyms. Empathy understands something of another's experience because of your own. Compassion is something different.

The definition of "compassion," from its Latinate roots, is "to suffer with." However, the biblical etymology of the word comes in the Hebrew from a word used to describe God's mercy: *rechem*, meaning "a mother's womb." Likewise, the New Testament Greek word for Jesus's compassion, *splagchnizomai*, means to be moved in the inward parts, i.e., the bowels. Being a woman, a mother, who has experienced both orgasm and childbirth, and a human who has experienced the function of the bowels, I understand all too well the involuntary nature of these functions. It is the very involuntariness of these acts that are physically connected to mercy and compassion in the ancient languages that I am drawn to remember when I consider compassion.

Compassion, unlike empathy, has nothing to do with what is known. Compassion is involuntary. Compassion comes upon you without intent. Thus, when you speak to someone who is devastated by a dark revelation about her spouse and you find yourself moved with mercy for her despite your cognitive judgment of the facts—that is compassion. When you stand in the room and watch your childhood friend reach for something to eat because of his involuntary need for food and without deliberation find yourself caring more about his dignity than being recognized as his old friend, that is compassion. When someone has disrespected you and you move on from your feeling of indignity because you can see the woundedness of the other though you have no knowledge of their experience—that is compassion. Gut-wrenching, bowel moving, birthing, involuntary response to another without intent or specific knowledge is the stuff of which compassion is made.

These days, we are too numb, overworked, wounded, asleep, and full of information even to find empathy for another living being, much less allow ourselves to be involuntarily moved by the suffering of another. We self-medicate, even perhaps meditate, to numb ourselves to our own suffering, the suffering of our fellow beings, and our Mother Earth. We don't even know the difference anymore between empathy and compassion, forgetting the roots of our language in the habits of common usage. We lose the depth of our languages, as well as the depth of our souls, our God-given ability to be moved involuntarily, to come alongside another the same way we are involuntarily moved to take our next breath. That is compassion.

Anyone want to pray for more?

3

Home/Loss and Gains

Soyinka Rahim

BIBO (beeboh) abbr: 1. a focused breath with sound, roar, sigh, hum, yum, shhhh 2. to release energy (roar, sigh) 3. to silence your thoughts or a room (shhhh) 4. to lighten your mood (hum) 5. to appreciate the good (yum) [English: BIBO from Soyinka Rahim, Grassroots Spiritual Practitioner]

Her face barely above water
Kicking, gasping for air
Praying to relax, trust, and float
The weight of fear, shame, sadness pulling her down
As she take action for her life to be a lantern of love
Pretending not to see, hear, feel the injustices
Sick from stolen culture, language, food, respect,
    self-confidence, family pride
Still she dance, sing, tell her stories
Keeping faith, creating new history
Giving herself permission to love
Her face barely above water
Kicking, gasping for air,

Standing tall, her spirit soaring
her face barely above water
Still gasping for air.

Nomad. Being of African American descent, ancestors sold and brought to America, considered livestock. This is her DNA, noticing and feeling how her people are being treated even today.

Gypsy. She's a member of a traveling group who tell their stories and hold sacred space for others to tell their stories. Open-minded and free-spirited.
She is dark skin with dark hair.

Faith Walker. Good, bad, ups, downs, disappointments, frustrations, she trusts the power of love/good/God.

Vagabond. She often will end up in places where her work is to wait for her next job.

Sojourner. She has many temporary stays.
She was pretty much homeless.

BIBO (Breathe in! Breathe out!)

She is from highway lust, daddy unknown.
Beauty, lupus, stepfather's wicked hands,
extension cords wrapped around thighs.

She is from love, beaded braids, homemade clothes, jewelry.
Mama's septum pierced, at 14, she pierced hers too.
Jam sessions, drums, flute, sax, stepfather on piano,
Mama singing.

She is from hustle, foods slung to walls,
sawed off shotgun, scared, women's
shelters, going home, again and again.

She is from camping, fishing, and peaches, cherries
picked from orchard, packed in sandwich bags,
for sale on the front porch for profit.

She is from hot water corn bread, black
beans, brown rice, collard greens, sweet potato
pie, honeydew melon, watermelon, fresh
squeezed orange juice, lemonade.

She is from German Shepherds, chickens
and a rooster, a big tee pee in the back,
tomatoes, weed, string beans, weed, corn on the cob,
weed, squash, onions, potatoes, fig tree, lemons,
apricots, kumquats.

She is from holistic thinking, afro-centric, power to
the people, world religion talk, spiritual practice.

She is from art and because she is a creation by the
creator she is a true manifestation of Love/Good/God.

BIBO (Breathe in! Breathe out!)

After her brother was murdered—cold case—and her mother transitioned out of body into the spirit world, she inherited her childhood home.

Oakland California, on the north side, since 1974.

She remembered the rainstorms in her childhood home,

buckets filling with water, rain hitting
the skylights making loud rattling sounds,
sometimes soft rhythmic sounds,
trees rustling, chimes resounding on the front porch
Mama's in the kitchen cooking, smelling too good,
Jazz music playing softly in the background.
Mama's painting on canvas, sewing and dancing,
Teaching her and her brother to bathe and
oil their bodies, from the top to the bottom, all about
    cleanliness.
Paying us to eat raw garlic for healthy blood, and to keep a
    strong immune system.

She was taught spiritual practices. Her mother told her that where the people were gathered in prayer for the good of humanity and the planet, she too could pray to help raise the Love/Good/God vibration.

Right in the midst of all the injustices, she would say, you too can pray, and where the people are gathered in prayer there are good people, and bad people, hand-in-hand, and that one decides to do bad, or to do good.

She was taught to build her altars, to meditate, create affirmations and to visualize what she wanted to manifest, but not fully understanding her spiritual powers, yet, that her mother so desperately wanted her to inhabit.

BIBO (Breathe in! Breathe out!)

In the mid-1960s, not too long after integration, most of the administrators and teachers in the school system were white, and the few black teachers had assimilated in such a way that if parents were raising their children differently from what was acceptable (like her mother giving her children African names), those parents and children were punished.

Which made it difficult for little black children and kids of color to become educated in the system that prepared them to work fast-food chains or assembly line jobs, or welfare recipients and desolate, and to separate men of color from their families.

Many times, she would hear her family talk about how blacks and people of color were not fighting for integration. We were and still are fighting for equality.

BIBO (Breathe in! Breathe out!)

She borrowed off the house to refurbish it. Her home needed major plumbing, electrical, roofing, replacing walls that had been removed. It was falling apart. She wanted to add a community art studio by extending the back of the house. She wanted more bedrooms in hopes that her family would be living in them.

She was working hard to make home a creative space, where family, folks, and friends, community could gather, and pray, play, and party, rest, bathe, cook, eat, dance, sing, chant, and share their stories.

She started her own community-based company, OURTHING Performing Arts Company, to perform an original modern-day folklore ballet that she conceived, choreographed, and directed entitled "An Altar Piece to Alter Peace" and to have a place where children could come for the summer, to play, pray, and party. She intended to celebrate the human experience, honoring our human-to-human connection, to the earth, wind, fire, water, and spirit-world birth, life, and death.

She was hoping to create a nuclear family for herself.

She met a man who told her she could get money out of her house by refinancing. He encouraged her to do that, multiple times, until she had a mortgage she could never afford.

BIBO (Breathe in! Breathe out!)

It was suggested that she sell or squat in her childhood home until she was put out. Those were her two options as far as she knew at the time.

She was recruited as a homeowner of color through a nonprofit organization that convinced her that they would help support folks to save their home. She was asked to stop payment by the nonprofit organization, to be six months in default, to qualify for the loan. She had never been late on her mortgage.

She stopped paying, then the organization was no longer available to help her, and the banks, who no longer knew who owned her loan, and she was not able to pay with all the money she had saved, in case something went wrong.

She had to sell her childhood home in 2010 because of bad choices that came from ignorance around home ownership, banks, and money.

Her whole neighborhood turned over in this period—all of the black families sold or lost their houses, and wealthier white families moved in. 1974, all young black families. 2015, all young white families. Then she remembered that throughout history communities of color had been gentrified. When the white men wanted the land, they would take it by any means necessary.

Gentrification by any means necessary. Lie, cheat, steal, trick. She got caught up with a socialized racist banking system that had been denying homes, land, and economic resources to people of color throughout history.

BIBO (Breathe in! Breathe out!)

She was determined to keep her mother's house. Knowing how much her mother went through to keep her family in a house, raising her children on welfare, living her life as a Renaissance woman, wife, mother, friend, and teacher to many, an artist, community-activist, spiritual practitioner.

She understands now on a deeper level the importance of listening to her spiritual helpers, trusting her internal voice, which is love/good/God. Remembering that her internal voice spoke to her many times saying over and over sell the house.

Awakening her from her sleep—sell the house.

Standing at the kitchen sink many times washing dishes and remembering watching, learning, and prepping food for her mother to cook, she would hear that internal voice—sell the house.

She would sometimes scream back at that voice. "No! This is my mother's house."

When those spiritual helpers came in body, and repeated the same thing, she was hearing from her internal voice—sell the house.

She could not hear them, because she felt alone and isolated, no mother, father, brother, sister, grandmother, grandfather, no aunties or uncles, no nuclear family.

She could not hear them.

BIBO (Breathe in! Breathe out!)

Her spiritual helpers rallied around her, protected her by not allowing her to go into debt nor walk away from her childhood home absolutely empty-handed. She sold her home.

She lost the land, the plants that her mother had grown in huge pots, family photographs, her mother's original art, old vinyl albums of jazz, blues, soul, pop, reggae, and her own Winnie the Pooh birthday album, tools to make jewelry, gold, silver, African trade beads, fabric, her mother's sewing machine, and many other material things in the move, some things she can't even remember.

She gained a higher spiritual consciousness.

After the big loss/gain, she became more committed to being a spiritual practitioner of love. She decided to live, to learn, to teach, to be love.

She coined BIBO (Breathe in! Breathe out!).

Sigh-release, relax, float, surrender, trust, believe; let it do what it do.

She believes we should create systemic love laws that will change our minds and strengthen the hearts of humanity so that we will better understand that there is enough matter for all of humanity.

She believes that we should love, honor, and respect our geographic, cultural gifts. We should distribute the resources as needed to nourish humanity and the planet, being committed to our authentic, true self, which is love, in all our human-to-human interaction.

She believes we should raise the human love frequencies, to vibrate the good.

BIBO—Breathe in! Breathe out! Love, stand, walk, speak, chant, sing, dance together to raise the vibration in the name of love/good/God, celebrate our creator, who created us to create, and choose to create joy, goodness, love, which is the heart and the soul of humanity.

She is committed to continuing to grow and have more compassion, better understanding that we are all works in progress, created by the creator to create, love/good/God, and to respect and honor each other and Mother Earth. Loving herself and giving herself permission to love and be loved. Deciding to be happy. Determined to be at home in her own skin.

She was able to get a deeper understanding of herself and her spiritual connection to the most high, trusting and believing in her ability to call forth her spiritual helpers in the crucial moments, in the name of love/good/God.

She continues to travel the world sharing her chants, songs, movement, dance, stories, and holding sacred space for the people. She is filled with gratitude to be asked to share her story, and to hold sacred space for others to dance sing/chant tell their stories.

Committed to reminding herself and others that each of us is responsible for feeding the love vessel, believing, knowing that it can expand, and to dismantle all the things that get in the way of the masterful creations of love/good/God.

Interplay became a platform in which she can continue to pray, play, party, and be a leader. A platform were she can celebrate her past experience as a performing artist, since the very beginning surrounded by art in her childhood home, dancing, singing, poetry, visual art, fashion shows, and music. She was young, beautiful, had a fabulous body, was talented and an insecure little girl. She facilitated her high school dance class, performed with her high school dance company as a featured dancer, taught at one of the most renowned dance studios in the Bay Area as a teenager, and performed with renowned African, Brazilian, modern, jazz dance companies.

Not knowing her worth she was "recruited" to dance overseas as a stripper—trafficked, sexualized, as many young girls and boys still are today.

After returning from overseas, she continued to perform and teach mindfulness, meditation, affirmation, visualization and rhythms, movements, chants, and songs to children in the Bay Area where she grew up, in the same educational system that failed her academically as a child.

When she found InterPlay, she found the eight principles that she chooses to live by.

1. Having an easy focus of weeeeeee! She knows having dis-ease creates disease so she must not let negative energy sit in her body.
2. Notice her body data, notice her patterns, and the choices she is making.
3. Trust her inner authority, believing what she is noticing, and understand she does not have to articulate an experience to have it.
4. Allow herself to have physicality of grace, notice the good, and have more singing, dancing, and quiet time.
5. She moves excess energy, having exformations, the opposite of information.
6. She knows in order to change her life she must change her practices, listening to her body wisdom.

7. Giving herself permission to go the speed of her body, one step, one moment, at a time the importance of incrementality.
8. Today she is able to name the good stuff in her life, creating affirmations.

Her workshop "Changing the Race Dance" uses movement, storytelling, and sound to engage the body, mind, heart, and spirit toward a global social movement for love, peace, community, and health.

She sees all of the colors of the rainbow—the black, brown, red, yellow, white—noticing who is in the room and who is not. When all these colors are mixed, we see black. We are all one.

She has opportunities to do "calls to gather" and opening rituals for organizations like Race Forward, which advances racial justice.

The people love her songs and chants. She's been told that they are prayers!

Her friends offered to produce a CD of her original music.

She knows that the spirit moves through her, shows her the rhythm to move through this world with love.

BIBO (Breathe in! Breathe out!)

She ordained herself as a GSP: Grassroots Spiritual Practitioner.

GSP—In the midst of so many names for God, she celebrates the love/good/God in all the gods and goddesses.

GSP—She honors that all life experiences are of God: the deaths of her loved ones, the gain and loss of material possessions, the fear of not matching her potential, or the heart-wrenching pain she felt when her lovers have left her or she chose to leave, or when she is suffering and feels absolutely alone in the world.

GSP—She asks all her judgments, critiques, and disapprovals, hate, greed take a backseat to love.

GSP—She is shining her light on love to dismantle all the -isms and religions that divide the people. She speaks out against the social norms that don't serve her people.

GSP—She calls upon the gods and goddesses. She believes that she can use her creative powers in a moment's time to redirect negative energy into a positive human experience.

GSP—She loves and is loved. She is committed to feeding the love vessel that runs through all beings.

GSP—She is willing to grow with the understandings and misunderstandings, truth and untruths, of her own personal experiences.

BIBO (Breathe in! Breathe out!)

She can hear her mother saying, "Life ain't nothing but something to do."

She's living because she's doing something.

She is working what she got, 'cause she got stuff: the joy, the good, the love, the most high.

Living the turtle life, one moment at a time.

She is spreading the BIBOLOVE. She makes home wherever she is.

4

"Breathe on Me, Lord;
I Can't Breathe"

ROSALIE NORMAN-MCNANEY

Breathe on me, Breath of God,
Fill me with life anew,
That I may love what Thou dost love,
And do what Thou wouldst do.
          —"Breath on Me, Breath of God" by Edwin Hatcher

F ocusing on one's breath is a way to become centered in the
moment so that we can be attentive to the moving of the Holy
Spirit within our lives. I usually begin a spiritual direction session
by inviting a directee to the practice as we begin a time of silence.
As we attend to each moment of inhalation and slow release, we
can experience the easing of the tension within our physical bodies and the scattered thoughts jostling within our minds. The spiritual discipline of focusing on our breath is also a reminder of God
breathing the breath of life into Adam and then to Eve bringing
forth life (Gen. 2:7).

So often we may go about the busyness of our day and neglect to pause to experience the gift of our breath, thus neglecting to heed the psalmist's words to "Be still, and know that I am God" as written in Psalm 46:10. Our nation has been reminded of the importance of human breath by those from whom the breath of life has been unjustly extinguished. In February 26, 2012, Trayvon Martin, a seventeen-year-old youth, was fatally shot by George Zimmermann in Sanford, Florida. Zimmermann was convinced that he had the right to carry a gun and to stop the breath of Travon who was Black and unarmed. The court affirmed his not guilty plea rather than punish his criminal actions against a youth whose breath had been snuffed out. Trayvon was unjustly profiled as dangerous because he was Black and wearing a hoodie in a neighborhood where Zimmerman thought Blacks did not belong.

Millions watched the actions of New York City police officers holding Eric Garner, forty-three, in a choke-hold on Staten Island on July 18, 2014. "I can't breathe," Garner gasped as officers held him down and repeatedly banged Garner's head on the hard pavement. Garner was arrested for resisting arrest and for allegedly selling untaxed cigarettes. Garner's body went lifeless, and he was dead on arrival (DOA) at the hospital. Eric Garner was also Black. On August 9, 2014, Michael Brown, an unarmed eighteen-year-old in Ferguson, Missouri, was shot by a white police officer who suspected the youth of a recent robbery and of carrying a weapon.

Freddie Gray died on April 21, 2015, as a result of unnecessary force used against him, resulting in a spinal cord injury after being arrested for allegedly carrying an illegal switch blade. Gray was not correctly secured inside a police van while being transported to the police station. Gray also said, "I can't breathe." It was later discovered that Gray did not have a switchblade, but instead a type of knife lawful to carry in Maryland: the type of knife that millions of men of all races carry every day throughout our nation. Unrest, protests, and riots broke out after each of the deaths of these Black youth and men. Each demonstration echoed loud and clear the same sentiment of injustice and violation of civil rights. Mothers, fathers, spouses, and children moan the loss of loved ones and we are shouting individually, corporately, and as a nation: I can't breathe; we can't breathe.

The violence and injustice we are facing today is far from the dream that the Rev. Dr. Martin Luther King Jr. spoke of on August 28, 1963. This is not the dream that would end racism and the inequality of Blacks and other minorities. Instead, there is a noose of injustice and racism cutting off the air of our Black youth and men. We have been jolted out of our dream to face a civil rights crisis and a complete reversal of what we had hoped would bring peace and new life. The breath of human beings is being cut off because of their color.

We may believe that Dr. King's dream has materialized in many ways. There are some changes of attitude and more opportunities toward inclusion, but there is still much more to be done. The recent violence against our Black youth and men has ignited the racial injustice conversation again. This is a pertinent conversation to get to the root of racism, which is a deep societal wound that has long been bandaged over and is essential for all of us. The worn bandages are peeling away and falling off as racism rises to the surface again in our society. These systems of racial injustice are being exposed in a legal system that unfairly tips the scales of justice in support of destroying our Black youth and men.

The "Stop and Frisk" practice allows a police officer to stop a suspicious individual and pat down the person's outer clothing to assess if the individual is carrying a weapon.[1] This is not a full-blown arrest and search. Its intent is crime prevention, so that police can act before there is probable cause. All of us want our communities protected. There was a time it was hoped that the police would be joint partners with their communities in maintaining civil liberties for all.

The reality is that there still exists a negative public view of African Americans and other racial groups and ethnicities. It is sadly assumed that African American men and other racial and ethnic groups are dangerous and are more likely to commit a crime. Neighborhoods are still structured to separate and to keep out the other, who are considered undesirable because of their physical characteristics or ethnicities. The media has long perpetuated the negative views about African Americans and specifically Black young men. This continues to cause a divide to the point that society does not distinguish between one person of color and another. Fear and suspicion is cast over all Blacks instead of seeing people as individuals. The portrayal of Blacks and minorities as dangerous, as demonstrated in the cases previously cited, profiles our Black and minority youth and men in a negative light.

---

1. See http://legal-dictionary.thefreedictionary.com/stop+and+frisk.

Michelle Alexander, social activist and author of *The New Jim Crow: Mass Incarnation in the Age of Colorblindness*,[2] uses the analogy of Jim Crow laws to show that the old racial caste system has been redesigned as a mass racial incarceration system for Blacks and Latinos. Alexander challenges the view that, by electing Barack Obama, a Black United States president, we are living in an era of colorblindness. Instead, Alexander speaks about the caste system that keeps our Black youth and men, and all minorities, disenfranchised through a racial incarceration caste system that relegates them to second-class citizenship. Alexander calls us all to action to bring about change.[3]

The root of the issue that must be addressed is the criminal justice system, and ultimately, our own attitudes need to be changed. We must move from marginalization to inclusion.

Take time to breathe and experience your breath as you exhale and know that we are all given the breath of life. Protesters against the violence and injustice in our nation are made up of all races, cultures, ethnicities, languages, and gender orientations. They have crossed state lines, racial and cultural borders, to come together to take a stand against prejudice, the violation of civil rights, and pronounce the claim that each person, regardless of race, has a right to breath.

The prophet Zephaniah, an Old Testament prophet who was of African descent, wrote about the remnant of people who were able to save a nation from God's wrath (Zeph. 3:11–13). Zephaniah's

---

2. Michelle Alexander, *The New Jim Crow: Mass Incarceration in the Age of Colorblindness* (New York: New Press, 2010).
3. Ibid.

message reminds us about a few humble people who trusted in the Lord and stood for truth. What is the truth? We are each created in God's image. In the book of Zephaniah, God sought to bring all people together, regardless of race, language, ethnicity, gender, and or age, beyond Jerusalem's borders to Ethiopia, as Jerusalem and the nations were given a new start in Zephaniah and all were gathered together (3:20) as "one" people before God. We can and must individually and corporately begin as a community of "One" made in God's image and valued as life brought forth by God again.

The Rev. Dr. Howard Thurman stated, "Community cannot feed for long on itself; it can flourish where always the boundaries are giving way to the coming of others from beyond them—unknown and undiscovered brothers."[4]

Denominations and faith communities have taken action. On December 8, 2014, The American Baptists USA called for an "examination of criminal justice" systems to address the continuing violence around us as a result of racism.[5] Episcopalians and others have taken similar stands.

As Christians believing that we are each made in the image of a loving God, we cannot turn away and breathe within our own safety zone. We are all affected, especially those of us who are Black and are of other racial ethnic groups—our sons, spouses, brothers, fathers, uncles, neighbors, friends, and coworkers. Rev. Dr. Martin

---

4. Howard Thurman, *A Strange Freedom: The Best of Howard Thurman on Religious Experience and Public Life*, ed. Walter Earl Fluker and Catherine Tumber (Boston: Beacon Press, 1998), 294.

5. ABC USA, "American Baptist Leaders Call for Examination of U.S. Criminal Justice System," December 18, 2014, http://www.abc usa.org/2014/12/08/american -baptist-leaders-call-for-examination-of-u-s-criminal-justice-systems/.

Luther King Jr. wrote from the Birmingham Jail, "Injustice any-where is a threat to justice everywhere."[6] This injustice has been the impetus for "Black Lives Matter": "Black Lives Matter is an ideological and political intervention in a world where Black lives are systematically and intentionally targeted for demise. It is an affirmation of Black folks' contributions to this society, our human-ity, and our resilience in the face of deadly oppression."[7]

I recently heard of a local church that displayed an outdoor sign with the words "Black Lives Matter." The next day the word "Black" was marked out and replaced with the word "All." The congregation, though surprised, would not be dismayed, and they replaced the sign, since their intent was to recognize and support Black Lives as being valued. The sign was their way to stand up to be counted as a congregation against the numerous senseless deaths of Black men by varied police forces across the country. They took steps so "all" could breathe. Their opponents sought to undermine the congregation's efforts by slashing out the word "Black," destroying the replaced sign until a third replacement sign was vandalized in its entirety.

"#BlackLivesMatter" doesn't mean the lives of persons who are not Black aren't important; it means that Black lives, which are seen as without value within a system of White supremacy, are important to your liberation. When Black people get free, everybody gets free. This is why we call on Black people and our allies to take up the call that Black lives matter. We're not saying Black lives are more important than other lives or that other lives are not criminalized

---

6. See https://kinginstitute.stanford.edu/king-papers/documents/letter-birmingham
-jail.
7. See blacklivesmatter.com/guiding-principles.

and oppressed in various ways. We remain in active solidarity with all oppressed people who are fighting for their liberation and we know that our destinies are intertwined.[8] And if we are committed to a world where all lives matter, we are called to support the very movement that inspired and activated so many more. That means supporting and acknowledging Black lives.

It also means that we are all called to set aside time to be prayerful about our role and responsibility in assuring that all lives and especially Black lives matter and one's life is not snuffed out as if their life didn't count. It means remembering that each human being is created in God's image and to negate a person's life because of his or her color is the same as negating God.

It means that we all must pause and consider what steps we can each take in advocating and providing justice for all. It means that, as we inhale the gift of the air surrounding us, we can exhale the hate and prejudice—that breath that restricts life in ourselves and in others.

It means that we are to act to ensure that our Black brothers and sisters deserve to breathe, live, and thrive, not just survive, on this earth and within our communities and nation.

Breath is God-given, and we are to continue to breathe and to fight for the breath of all.

> Breathe on me, Breath of God,
> Until my heart is pure,
> Until with Thee I will one will,
> To do and to endure.

---

8. Ibid.

God has instilled breath into all, and we are made in God's image.

Breathe on us, dear God, individually and corporately, so that we may be your witnesses against institutions and individuals that are perverted by racism.

Lord, help us to be new. Breathe on us, God. Breathe courage and peace within, and instill in us the willingness to breathe out the racism that has hold of our country and bring new life. Help us to be free from our own biases and to be reconciled through Jesus Christ. Move us to peaceful actions that bring about change, so that we can breathe the breath of New Life.

5

Love and Kenosis: Contemplative Foundations of Social Justice

Gigi Ross

L ove. Contemplation and action begin with love. Contemplation and action end with love. What connects the two and makes them one is love. And the love linking and undergirding contemplation and action is the foundation of social justice.

Jesus links contemplation and action in three subtly deeper ways in the Synoptic Gospels of Matthew, Mark, and Luke, each time combining love of God as stated in the Jewish *Shema*, Deuteronomy 6:5, and love of neighbor from the Holiness Code of Leviticus 19. I begin by contemplating the reality of Jesus's words on contemplation—love of God—and social action—love of neighbor.

Jesus Speaks on Contemplation and Action

In Matthew 22:34–40, a lawyer tests Jesus by asking which commandment in the law—there are 613 of them—is the greatest. Jesus answers, "You shall love the Lord your God with all your heart, and with all your soul, and with all your mind." This, in essence, is con-templation: being completely present in love to God and fully open to God's loving presence within.

It turns out the greatest commandment is not one but two. Jesus continues his response equating loving your neighbor as yourself with loving God fully and completely. Then he concludes, "On these two hang all the law and the prophets." The prophets were the voice of social justice in Jesus's day. For Jesus, trying to obey the commandments or follow the words of the prophets without being rooted and grounded in love is as impossible as a cloud trying to retain water. Clouds must release the water they are. God's commandments can only be carried out in the love that is their source.

In Mark 12:28–34, it's not a lawyer who comes to test Jesus, but someone who combines legal and theological knowledge. The scribe's question is slightly different than the lawyer's: "Which com-mandment is the first of all?" Unlike the querent in Matthew, he was not simply seeking a comparison but also wanting to know about beginnings and sources. "In keeping the commandments, where do we begin?" or "What is the original commandment?" are other ways he could have phrased his question, depending on the level of meaning he wished to draw out. As we'll see in his response to Jesus, this scribe understood and appreciated nuanced and mul-tivalent expression.

This time Jesus replies with the entire *Shema* beginning with "Hear, O Israel: the LORD is our God, the LORD alone." Oneness is where Jesus begins his response, and his answer ends with one-ness. God is one, so God's greatest commandment is not only two but one. You love God as one, and you are one with your neighbor in love.

The scribe's affirmation—"You are right"—implies he knew the answer before he asked. He then glosses Jesus's response, confirming that God is one and adds there is no other besides God—another statement with multiple levels of meaning—and that love—loving God with one's whole being (contemplation), loving others as oneself (action)—"is much more important than all whole burnt offerings and sacrifices." This assertion tells me the scribe's query begged for a qualitative response about origin rather than a quantitative one about rank because although the laws regarding burnt offerings, sacrifices, and matters related to the temple and temple service far outnumber the other laws Jews of Jesus's day were required to observe, they were of lesser importance. Jesus, acknowledging the scribe's wisdom, concludes, "You are not far from the kingdom of God."

The test question in Luke 10:25–28 concerns life rather than law. "What must I do to inherit eternal life?" Jesus sometimes used "eternal life" as a synonym for "kingdom of God," so this question seems related to Jesus's comment that the scribe in Mark was not far from the kingdom of God. And yet, in reply, Jesus points the lawyer to the law, asking what is written there. The lawyer repeats the words about loving God and neighbor that Jesus used in Matthew and Mark. Jesus, echoing the scribe in Mark, points the lawyer back to life. "You have given the right answer, do this, and you will live." Jesus is not talking about life as an inheritance or future possession but life as something to be lived now. Eternal life is loving God and neighbor now. Living is contemplation and action.

How Jesus Lives Contemplation and Action

How do we do this, live this love? How did Jesus live it? *Kenosis*. *Kenosis* is a word taken from the Greek, a variant of which is used by Paul when he exhorts the Philippians to have the same mind as Christ Jesus

> who, though he was in the form of God,
> > did not regard equality with God
> > as something to be exploited,
> but emptied himself,
> > taking the form of a slave,
> > being born in human likeness.
> And being found in human form
> > he humbled himself
> > and became obedient to the point of death—
> > even death on a cross.
> Therefore God also highly exalted him
> > and gave him the name
> > that is above every name. (Phil. 2:6–9)

The word "emptied," a translation of the Greek word *ekenōse*, describes the mind with which Jesus loved God and neighbor, with which we are called to contemplation and action.

This mindset is not fixed but a process, a dance that unfolds as follows: a loving recognition of oneness or unity or union with God, letting that recognition go, allowing the sense of separateness to arise, letting it die, allowing the resurrection of the sense of oneness with God, letting it go to repeat the cycle. Readers who practice meditations like Centering Prayer or Vipassanā may recognize this cycle.

For Jesus, living contemplation and action begins with oneness, "The Lord our God is one," "though he was in the form of God." This union is ultimately the fruit of loving God. Contemplation is loving God.

Christ did not cling to equality with God nor use this union to his advantage. He "did not regard equality with God as something to be exploited, but emptied himself." He surrendered his divinity, his power, his privilege, his . . . until there was no "his," nothing to call his own, nothing to possess, nothing.

Christ became poor and human, unworthy to be born inside a home. He was born with the animals, as if he were a slave, beyond the acknowledgement of those more privileged. In letting go of his low status and humanity, Jesus "became obedient unto death," experiencing complete separation from God when he cried, "My God, my God, why have you forsaken me?" The Latin root of "obedient" is *oboedire* from *ob*, "in the direction of," and *audire*, "hear." In letting go of divinity and humanity, Jesus continued to listen, his hearing oriented to God's command. And, for Jesus, that command is love.

Jesus completely let go of his human identity and in doing so, he realized his divinity. "Therefore God also highly exalted him and gave him the name that is above every name." The name that is above every name is God's name. Christ becomes one with God again.

This is how Jesus lived contemplation and action. He emptied himself. Love filled the space. He emptied himself. Fear filled the space. He emptied himself. He was hungry. He did not turn stones into bread. He emptied himself.

Kenosis is Jesus's way. It is also the way of followers of Jesus. Paul challenges us to have the same attitude Jesus had, to continually let go of our identity. Simha Bunam, a rabbi in the Hasidic tradition, says each of us must have two pockets into which we reach as needed. In one pocket are the words, "For my sake the world was created," and in the other, "I am earth and ashes."[1] Rabbi Bunam is referring to our divinity and humanity. In both the Jewish and Christian traditions, humans are the end for which everything was created. More mystical strands of these traditions recognize us as the consciousness of the universe, as God's hands and feet, in the words of Teresa of Avila.[2] We are also dust and ashes, capable of extreme cruelty, and attracted to much that is trivial. So we are called to let go of our divinity and humanity, our nobility and servility, our integrity and dishonesty, and ultimately our images of God and ourselves. This is the way of *kenosis* that allowed Jesus to love God and neighbor unconditionally as he served as a vessel through which God's love flowed into the world.

Living the Kenotic Life

How is this kenotic path lived today? Varied are the ways of *kenosis*. Each person's path is unique. As I live into my own path of

---

1. Martin Buber, "Two Pockets," in *Tales of the Hasidim: Book Two: The Later Masters,* trans. Olga Marx (1947; New York: Schocken Books, 1975), 249–50.
2. See Teresa of Avila, "You are Christ's Hands," in *The Longing in Between: Sacred Poetry from Around the World,* ed. Ivan M. Grangerm (Boulder, CO: Poetry Chaikhana, 2014), 160.

contemplation and action, I've been inspired by people currently living kenotic lives. African American environmentalist John Francis is one of them.

John Francis

In January 1971, two oil tankers collided, leaking 840,000 gallons of their cargo into the San Francisco Bay. As with many of his neighbors, the spill sparked in John Francis thoughts of living more lightly, consuming less oil. But they were only thoughts. They led to no lifestyle change.

Several months later, a good friend of his died in a motor boat accident. In celebration of his life John and his partner Jean walked twenty miles to a nightclub to dance. They walked twenty miles back. And John continued walking. For twenty-two years he gave up riding in motorized vehicles.

His *kenosis* didn't end there. He gave up smoking cigarettes and marijuana. Because he no longer drove, he became an ineffective band manager and was fired. The night before his birthday, he slept outside on the mesa and reflected on his life. As much as he knew walking was right for him, he was not happy. He could tell by the arguments he had with people who offered him rides and were offended when he refused. For his birthday, he gave his community the gift of his silence. If he was not talking, how could he get into arguments? He learned so much about himself on his birthday he continued his silence day after day for seventeen years.

Near the end of his memoir *Planetwalker*, John Francis reflects on what he couldn't have known when he began his kenotic path:

If twenty years ago, after witnessing an oil spill in San Francisco Bay, someone had told me, "John, if you want to make a difference, I want you to stop driving and start walking east, and you'll make a difference," and as I turned and walked away they shouted, "and shut up, too!" I would not have believed them.[3]

Impossible as it sounds, walking and silence led to a love for the environment and an understanding that we humans are the environment and how we treat each other impacts the environment. This understanding is foundational to environmental justice, awareness of our oneness with the environment and loving our neighbor the environment as ourselves.

With this love and understanding, in 1983, John Francis began a seven-year walk across the United States. Along the way, he stopped in Oregon for two years to study for his bachelor's degree in science and mathematics with a concentration in biology and a creative writing minor. He spent another two years in Montana getting his master's in environmental studies, and he studied another two years for his PhD in land resources from the Institute for Environmental Studies at the University of Wisconsin. He was the only person researching and writing about the costs and legalities of managing oil spills when the Exxon Valdez struck a reef and leaked over 11 million gallons of oil into Alaska's Prince William Sound on March

---

3. John Francis, *Planetwalker: How to Change Your World One Step at a Time* (Point Reyes Station, CA: Elephant Mountain Press, 2005), 274. Republished in 2009 by the National Geographic Society as *Planetwalker: 22 Years of Walking, 17 Years of Silence.*

24, 1989. At the time, it was the largest oil spill in US waters. His dissertation led to a job in Washington, DC, with the United States Coast Guard writing regulations for the Oil Pollution Act of 1990, legislation drafted in direct response to the Exxon Valdez accident.

John Francis channels his work championing environmental justice through his nonprofit Planetwalk, which creates many projects and originates a curriculum for environmental education. He has served as United Nations Environmental Programme Goodwill Ambassador to the World's Grassroots Communities, promoting global awareness of environmental issues and the work of the UN Environmental Programme. From 2010–2013, he was in the first group of education fellows at the National Geographic Society, and at the time of this writing, he is a visiting associate professor at the University of Wisconsin, where he received his PhD. He teaches graduate and undergraduate seminars in environmental studies. For John Francis, making a difference in how people value and treat the environment was as easy as giving up riding in motorized vehicles and talking.

Of course, it wasn't easy and he couldn't have done it alone. His kenotic life was made possible because emptying himself included letting go of independence and learning to live interdependently, just as Jesus relied on others, often women, to support his ministry. As John Francis walked across the country, studying and sharing his message, Bay Area friends would meet him and bring supplies, or people he met along the way would give him a meal, a place to stay, a donation. Having the same mind as Christ Jesus, there were also times when he remained obedient unto death.

Returning from his first long walk, five hundred miles from Inverness, California, to the Kalmiopsis Wilderness in Oregon, John Francis watched a truck pass him and stop just ahead. The driver, calling him "boy," motioned him over, asked where he was going, and pulled out a gun.

"We don't like niggers around here," the driver said and pulled the trigger. The gun did not fire. John Francis backed away. The truck was driven away. In all that time, John did not speak but used gestures to communicate. John writes about the rest of the walk:

> On my way down to Highway One I pass through the fog. After the warmth of the sun it sends a chill up my spine. I am both angry and afraid. Angry that life can still take such an ugly and familiar form, and afraid that death will catch me before I get home. I begin to shiver uncontrollably.
>
> When I reach the highway some friends from Point Reyes are driving by. They stop and we embrace. They tell me that reports of my progress coming down the coast have been reaching home. I am so happy to see them that I begin to cry, big silent tears through a silly smile. They look worried and ask if I am all right. I hesitate and then nod yes, but for a moment I think of getting into the car with them where I can be safe. But there is too much for me to express standing there beside the highway. I can only wave to them as they drive on up the coast.[4]

---

4. Ibid., 60.

John Francis began talking again on Earth Day, April 22, 1990, and about two years later he was riding in all kinds of motorized vehicles. As Jesus emptied himself of his identity, John Francis emptied himself of his image as the silent walker. Now his life embraces talking and being silent, riding in motorized vehicles and going for extended walks, a kenotic cycle that clings to no one way.

Giving up that identity didn't come easy. Every year on his birthday he asked himself whether he should continue his silence. Because of that annual discernment he knew when to empty himself of silence. But he had no such process for discerning when to end his walking. It took an argument with an armed guard outside a Venezuelan prison to realize walking was no longer life-giving but left him empty, feeling like a prisoner. His attachment to walking no matter what had begun to stop the flow of love for himself and others. The time had come for that identity to die and for the resurrection of a new one.

My Experience of Kenosis

Death to resurrection. Divinity to humanity. Independence to interdependence. Having a job, a title, an identity to being unemployed, in poverty, with no accepted or understandable identity. Cycles of kenosis.

Kenosis came to me unbidden when I lost my full-time job in 2008 and ran out of money a year later. It came tasting like betrayal, a setup. The job I'd been given was a perfect fit where I lived my call fully, did everything right and well, and then the ground opened up beneath me. Even though I had an intuition

47

I would be asked to empty myself of my position and the identity I'd attached to it, this kenosis was not what I wanted. And when the time came to leap into the abyss, my unvoiced "yes" was not wholehearted. The six-year experience of unemployment, poverty, and homelessness that followed stripped me of my willfulness to try to make something happen and filled me with knowing how utterly I am loved by God, by the Universe. This awareness became apparent only when I loved others as I am loved, not just unconditionally but kenotically, with a love that is not mine but which flows through me as I empty myself of expectations, agendas, self-interest, and identity.

As with John Francis, that love came in the form of a community to support me on my path and people I met along the way who gave me meals, money, and leads to places to stay. Thanks to this community of God's hands and feet, I did not spend one night on the street nor have a day with nothing to eat. The corollary to loving your neighbor as yourself is to allow your neighbor to love you. To allow myself to be loved and be dependent on others meant staying empty, and living this empty left me open as a conduit for God's love in ways I couldn't imagine.

In my last year of living in poverty, I spent two months catsitting in a condominium in a suburb just outside of Washington, DC. At the time, the owner needed a cat sitter, and I needed a place to stay. Meeting my need for a place to stay allowed this mother to accompany her son to Johns Hopkins Hospital in Baltimore, where she donated bone marrow for his bone marrow transplant. Having someone stay with her cats saved her added worry about the cats' welfare and the cost of boarding them with someone or a facility, enabling her to devote more energy into being present to her son and to her part in his healing.

The most difficult time of this period, the kenosis of kenosis for me, was the twenty months I stayed with an activist in her eighties in exchange for helping her continue to live independently in her two-bedroom apartment. She had several chronic health problems and her cognition was noticeably declining. She also regularly participated in protests—against the military's use of drones; Bradley, now Chelsea, Manning's arrest, trial, and sentencing; and Wells Fargo Bank's financing of for-profit prisons, for example. She had set up a trust fund to give away most of her money to charitable nonprofit organizations and her church, keeping just enough for essentials, including rent for an apartment in a building for low-income seniors.

My stay was difficult because the day-to-day details that were my responsibilities mattered less and less to her, and it became more difficult for her to understand the necessity of taking care of them. Secondly, the room where I stayed shared a wall with the apartment next door. The neighbor's television was always on and always loud. I did not sleep well. Poor sleep colored my ability to be present to the woman I was supposed to help.

Six months into my stay everything came to a head. Unexpected cleaning to be done yet again on my day off. An argument. Angry shouts. Later conversation about what happened. Not remembering my hurtful words. Once reminded, a vague memory, my wake-up call.

I saw a side of myself that shocked me. I reflected on why I couldn't remember what I knew I had said. I continued my pondering in prayer and spiritual direction. I promised myself never again to take my stress out on her, but to keep it between me and God, who could take my anger without being hurt or thinking ill of me. I only discussed my discomfort with my spiritual director and my closest friends. For broadcasting my irritation too widely would have kept it alive through repeated attention, and I wouldn't have had a prayer of emptying myself of my anger. Talking about it too much would have made it more difficult to keep my promise.

I kept my promise and lived there fourteen months more with further opportunities to empty myself. The noise next door continued. I rarely got a good night's sleep or quiet during my morning prayer time. There was no magic wand I could have waved to make myself comfortable. It made as much sense to ask my neighbor to turn down her television as to ask an albatross not to soar. She was hard of hearing, and she liked to watch television. I wasn't going to interfere with how she spent her time.

The time came to empty myself of this living situation. The woman I was staying with began asking me to do more and more things she used to do. Eventually, it became clear that remaining in the apartment would no longer help her live independently. Fortunately for me, just as I was discerning this, a six-month house-sitting opportunity arose.

Conclusion

So how does my kenotic life relate to social justice? It's easy to see the relationship between John Francis's kenosis and his work for environmental justice. But what does my kenosis have to do with justice?

I'm still living into the answer. I see an obvious connection to social justice when I was helping the activist participating in protests in the name of justice. But the connection goes deeper. I started this essay describing contemplation and social action as aspects of love, and love as the foundation of social justice. This view of love is not original with me. Martin Luther King Jr., to name one among a host of witnesses, writes in *Stride Toward Freedom* about discovering this same connection through Gandhi's example of *Satyagraha*, which he translated as truth or love force.[5] I've shown how for Jesus all of God's commandments come down to love. The major fruit of my time of kenosis was a deepening of my capacity to love. To love strangers, to love in discomfort, to love in the unknowing. While I was learning to love kenotically, God's love flowed to others: a social activist in her eighties, a mother with her son who was battling a terminal illness, their cats.

Not only is love the source of contemplation, but contemplation deepens our awareness of love and of God who is love. For Parker Palmer, an educator and activist, the goal of contemplation is "to help us see through the deceptions of self and world in order to get in touch with what Howard Thurman called 'the genuine' within us and around us."[6] He continues writing that contemplation can be

---

5. See Martin Luther King Jr., *Stride Toward Freedom* (San Francisco: Harper and Row, 1986), 96–97.
6. Parker J. Palmer, "Contemplative By Catastrophe," On Being with Krista Tippett (blog), November 11, 2015, https://onbeing.org/blog/contemplative-by -catastrophe/.

defined in terms of function: *"Contemplation is any way one has of penetrating illusion and touching reality."*[7] With this definition, we return to Burghardt's "long, loving look at the real." The long, loving look at the reality of my anger with the activist I stayed with was contemplation. I took my anger to God out of love for her and myself, and, in doing so, deepened my love for her and for me. This contemplation emptied me of my anger without removing the stress of that living situation, yet I was empty enough to serve in love.

My kenosis of status and home underscored my solidarity with others who live on the margins of cultural norms and expectations. Here is where I find the beginnings of an answer to how my six-year experience relates to justice. As John Francis learned that we are the environment, so I learned that I am marginalized, but not just me. We are all marginalized in some way. This solidarity is the essence of loving your neighbor as yourself. It leads to the discovery that your neighbor is yourself. Interdependence becomes communion. The two commandments become one. Loving my neighbor as myself is loving God with my whole being. God loved is neighbor loved.

My kenosis experience was a lived experience of being on the margins. That solidarity with the marginalized was affirmed in my interactions with other homeless people, some of whom commented on my "realness." This sense of communion informs my open, prayerful listening in spiritual direction. It helps shape projects I work on. My lived understanding of interdependence infuses

---

7. Ibid (emphasis in the original).

my current work at the Center for Action and Contemplation, an organization dedicated to supporting the contemplative dimension of social justice.

May I continue living this love as the next leg of kenosis unfolds in a new city and in new work. May we all grow in our love of God and neighbor as we seek to support the reign of justice in our corner of the earth.

6

"Pray for Yourself"

Vikki Montgomery

Pray for yourself."

I had been ranting about and railing against someone who had hurt me deeply. I felt betrayed and angry. I listed all of her sins: all the things she had done to me—and to everyone else—from the day we met. I mused aloud that the friendship was over. How could I possibly be a friend with a person like this?

My spiritual director listened quietly. I thought she was being empathetic, so I continued to list the transgressions of my friend against me. I declared, "I will have to pray for her to get over this."

That's when my spiritual director interjected, "Pray for yourself."

Stunned, I looked at her in disbelief. A few minutes went by. I started in again.

"Pray for yourself," she repeated.

It rang in my ears. It didn't penetrate my heart. She had said this to me in other contexts. "Pray for yourself about your call." "Pray for yourself about your desires." "Pray for yourself about your health." Never a simple, "Pray for yourself."

It stung a bit. Why should I pray for myself? How could I be the problem? I was the one who had been hurt. I was the one who had been loyal. I was the one who had tried to help my friend from the beginning.

Then it dawned on me. The problem wasn't with my friend. The problem was with *me*. I was the Christian. I was the one who had sought spiritual direction eleven years before to deal with a life full of hurts. I was the one who wanted to get better and to do better.

Instead, I was wallowing in the hurts I (thought I) had gotten over. New information about an old betrayal had made everything feel raw and new again. I felt as immersed in the pain as when I first entered spiritual direction.

My spiritual director saw the signs. She gently but firmly brought me back to the present. Back into the strength in which she had seen me grow. Back to the forgiveness I had rendered to those who had hurt me. Back to the mandate to Jesus's followers to bless *and* to pray for those who hurt us (Luke 6:28).

But it came with a twist: "Pray for yourself."

I remember thinking, was that even biblical? The closest I could get was the command, "Do not judge, so that you may not be judged" (Matt. 7:1). It occurred to me that I was judging my friend while I was railing against her. I was listing all of her faults and wrongs. I was questioning her motives. Our friendship. Our trust. The betrayal felt real, but so was my judgment against her.

Then I asked myself, would I want someone to talk about me as I was talking about her? In horror, I asked myself, was that loving? Wasn't that what I was called to do as a Christian—to love? Furthermore, was I loving her as I loved myself? The second great commandment pierced my consciousness, "You shall love your [friend] as yourself" (Matt. 22:39).

The first, "You shall love the Lord your God with all your heart, and with all your soul, and with all your mind," wasn't far behind in my memory (Matt. 22:37). If I loved God with everything in me—heart, soul, and mind—how could I have space for disparaging someone else no matter how badly that person hurt me?

Obviously, I needed to look at love again and how to respond as a Christian when a person acts in an unloving way toward me. I needed to look at prayer again, and most of all, I needed to learn again to pray for myself.

Weeks later, it hit me. The Lord's Prayer. That's the model. I remembered what the original twelve disciples said to Jesus, after observing him in prayer: "Teach us to pray."

After I whispered, "Teach me to pray for myself," I started repeating the prayer.

Our Father in heaven,
hallowed be your Name,[1]
your kingdom come,
your will be done,
on earth as in heaven.

---

1. This version of the Lord's Prayer is taken from Daily Morning Prayer: Rite II in the *The Book of Common Prayer*, accessed last on December 16, 2015, http://www.episcopalchurch.org/files/downloads/book_of_common_prayer.pdf, or from *The Book of Common Prayer and the Administrations of the Sacraments and Other Rites and Ceremonies of the Church, Together with the Psalter or Psalms of David, According to the use of The Episcopal Church* (New York: Church Publishing, 2007), 97.

I stumbled, and then stopped. So far in the prayer it was all about praying *to* God *about* God. Nothing had been about anyone else. I started from the top and continued,

Give us today our daily bread.

That's about me, I thought. I repeated these phrases again and again from the beginning up to that point as I puzzled it out. The next time, I continued to the next line.

Forgive us our sins

Yes. Forgive me for being so hard on my friend. For avoiding her. For resenting her. For being angry at her. For my inability to engage with her. For not being able to let it go. For letting it consume me. For not being able to forgive her.

I circled back to the beginning and continued.

. . . as we forgive

That stopped me. As we forgive. While, when, whenever, because, during, before, after, always. I had asked for forgiveness, but I was reminded that it seemed to have a condition. I might only ask forgiveness as I *give* forgiveness. I tried to say it again:

as we forgive those who sin against us.

Seven lines in and only now was I involving someone else other than God and me. And there was really only one word referring to that other person (or persons), *those*. *Those* translated into "she." My friend.

I had to say the prayer up to this point again using "me" and "my" rather than "us" and "our" to feel the impact of this new understanding.

With sixty-two words in the prayer before "Amen," I had to pray thirty-three words before mentioning anyone else. Then these thirty-three words were followed by the four crucial words: *"who sin against us."* It didn't even warrant a whole line. Just a phrase: *"those who sin against us."*

Who else are *those*, I mused? Everybody? Strangers? Neighbors? Colleagues? Family? Friends? Of course, my friend.

It became less personal and more personal at the same time. I became more aware of why Jesus taught the prayer using communal language. It's not just about me and my problem with my friend. It's about how I engage with all the people around me.

I had been saying the prayer at least once a day for years—recently, twice and at least three times on monastic retreats when praying the Offices. How did I miss the importance of this? Rather than dwelling on an answer, I looked back at the scriptural passages about the prayer.

There are two. Luke 11:1–4 when the disciples asked for instruction in prayer. Matthew 6:9–14, where Jesus was discussing prayer in general, really struck me. Not only did Jesus talk about prayer and give the model, he emphasized the need for forgiveness.

"And forgive us our debts, as we also have forgiven our debtors," Jesus said in Matthew 6:12. Then he finished the prayer, he explained the *why* of forgiveness and the holy transaction that occurs, in verses 14–15:

For if you forgive others [italics mine] their trespasses, your heavenly Father will also forgive you; *but if you do not* forgive others, neither will your Father forgive your trespasses.

In Mark 11:25 (which was actually the first Gospel written), first Jesus gave a command then described the transaction:

Whenever you stand praying, forgive, if you have anything against anyone; so that your Father in heaven may also forgive you your trespasses.

In the prior verse he was telling the disciples that if they believed, their prayers would be answered. But he added a caveat: You have to forgive others to be heard. Jesus was saying: drop everything and take care of this before you go any further.

Although what we call the Lord's Prayer appears in only two Gospels, this instruction on forgiveness appears in all four. John recounts the last time Jesus repeats the instruction on forgiveness. After his resurrection, Jesus visits the believers hidden away in a room. He breathes the Holy Spirit upon them and reminds them immediately,

If you forgive the sins of any, they are forgiven them; if you retain the sins of any, they are retained. (John 20:23)

I say condition and caveat loosely, because it isn't about a simple exchange or a quid pro quo. It's about a relationship. Our *un*-forgiveness gets in the way of our relationship with God.

It's like inviting a loquacious third party on a date with your beloved and seating that person between you and yours. You can't concentrate on the person you're supposed to be with because your attention is distracted and divided by that other person's chattiness.

Your beloved can't concentrate on you or get a word in because that person is always talking, and your beloved is nonverbally asking several questions about that other person's presence. (Who is this person? What is this person doing here? Why did you invite whoever-it-is? Are you trying to tell me something?)

There is no chance to deepen the relationship with your beloved. There is no way for the two of you to be physically close because the noisy person is in the middle.

The evening is a bust. You are unsatisfied with your decision. Your beloved is unhappy. Your relationship is strained. If it happens again, your relationship will continue to devolve. But the noisy person is oblivious and unaffected. Only you and the beloved suffer.

I was suffering. My friend, not so much—yet. God and I. Yes. I think God was in pain for me in my pain. I was shutting off myself from God's healing. That's not how love is supposed to work. That's not how forgiveness is supposed to work.

As I was working through these ideas, I thought about my ancestors and heroes and sheroes of the civil rights movement. They couldn't afford to allow their hurts, pain, resentments, or emotions to lead them into actions that would jeopardize their lives. I particularly thought about my personal hero, John Lewis, the congressman who has represented Georgia's 5th District since 1986. He was a Freedom Rider, a founder of the Student Nonviolent Coordinating Committee, the last of the "Big Six" of the civil rights movement, a speaker at the March on Washington, and a protégé of the Rev. Dr. Martin Luther King Jr.

Lewis has been called the "conscience of the U.S. Congress."[2] I know he worked deliberately to educate his conscience. He tells of his training in "the way of nonviolence"[3] led by James Lawson, a minister and a field secretary of the Fellowship of Reconciliation (an organization that has been working for peace, justice, and nonviolence since 1915[4]). Lawson taught members of Nashville's Student Movement (a precursor to SNCC) how to respond in love.

Lawson was a contemporary of the Rev. Dr. Martin Luther King Jr., who had urged him to postpone college and join the movement. Lawson had spent time as a missionary in India, where he had studied Gandhi's philosophy and tactics. While a student at Vanderbilt Divinity School, he helped prepare area undergraduate students for their sit-ins at segregated businesses and for Freedom Rides.

Lewis wrote about how they practiced responding by role-playing. Some would play the bad guys and others the students, then switch:

> It was not enough, [Jim Lawson] would say, simply to endure a beating. It was not enough to resist the urge to strike back at an assailant. "That urge can't *be* there," [Lawson] would tell us. "You have to do more than just not hit back. You have to have no *desire* to hit back. You have to *love* that person who's hitting you."[5]

---

2. "Biography," Congressman John Lewis: Representing Georgia's 5th District, accessed December 4, 2015, https://johnlewis.house.gov/john-lewis/biography.

3. John Lewis, *Walking with the Wind: A Memoir of the Movement* (New York: Simon & Shuster, 1998), 77.

4. Fellowship of Reconciliation, accessed December 16, 2015, http://forusa.org/.

5. Lewis, *Walking,* 85 (italics in the original).

He said Lawson taught them a specific technique to use:

> Imag[ine] that person—actually *visualize* him or her—as an
> infant, as a baby. If you can see this full-grown attacker who
> faces you as the pure innocent child that he or she once
> was—that we *all* once were—it is not hard to find compas-
> sion in your heart. It is not hard to find forgiveness. And
> this, Jim Lawson taught us, is at the essence of the nonvio-
> lent way of life—the capacity to forgive.[6]

Lewis called it a way of life on which Lawson wanted them to
embark:

> his is not simply a technique or a tactic or a strategy or a
> tool to be pulled out when needed. It is not something you
> turn on or off like a faucet. This sense of love, this sense of
> peace, the capacity for compassion, is something you carry
> inside yourself every waking minute of the day. It shapes
> your response to a curt cashier in the grocery store or to a
> driver cutting you off in traffic just as surely as it keeps you
> from striking back at a state trooper who might be kicking
> you in the ribs because you dared to march in protest.[7]

Still Lewis was not a Pollyanna, believing that if they had enough
love everything would change instantly. He believed change would
happen through working through conflicting emotions.

---

6. Ibid., 77 (italics in the original).
7. Ibid.

I have always believed there is room for both outrage and anger *and* optimism and love. Many, many times in my life, in many situations and circumstances, I have felt all these emotions at once. I think this is something that separated me from many of my colleagues in SNCC—the fact that they saw this struggle as an either/or situation, that they believed it was impossible to feel hope and love at the same time as you felt anger and a sense of injustice.[8]

This difference in perspective, he continued, played out in the years following the sit-ins. Lewis found himself betrayed and pushed out of the organization he helped found by people he considered friends. I could relate to that.

These thoughts coalesced in the weeks following my conversation with my spiritual director. Beyond my own hurt, from someone I considered a friend, I thought about how I would respond to someone who had intentionally tried to harm me, or, as Lewis mentioned, someone in a store or in traffic who was simply careless with my feelings or body. I had cringed as I read it. If I gave myself permission to disparage a friend, how might I react to a stranger?

How many times had my daughters pointed out my road rage when driving in downtown DC traffic? (Truth: I was terrified of the other drivers—especially the taxi drivers who would suddenly do a U-turn on a rain-slick, two-way street—the ones who cut me off, causing me to slam on my brakes hard enough to give myself a headache, the ones who rattled me by honking because I was confused by a traffic circle, and the others who rolled down their

---

8. Ibid., 230–31 (italics in the original).

windows to yell at me.) How often had I exchanged unpleasantries with harried service people? Did I really want to revisit the times I had been rude to people who weren't up to my standards?

I concluded that I did need to pray for myself. Things inside me were still messy, despite my profession of loving God and neighbor. I was reminded of the story that author, poet, mystic, and preacher Howard Thurman told about a white man talking to him about his sons:

> I am rearing my boys so that they will not hate Negroes. Do not misunderstand me. I do not love them, but I am wise enough to know that if I teach my boys to hate Negroes, they will end up hating white people as well.[9]

Thurman ended the story by writing: "Hatred cannot be controlled once it is set in motion."[10] Earlier in the chapter, Thurman discussed all the things hate does: "destroys the core of the life of the hater," "guarantees a final isolation from one's fellows," "blinds the individual to all values of worth," "cannot be confined to the offenders alone."[11] And most important:

> Jesus rejected hatred because he saw that hatred meant death to the mind, death to the spirit, death to communion with his Father. He affirmed life, and hatred was the great denial.[12]

---

9. Howard Thurman, *Jesus and the Disinherited* (Boston: Beacon Press, 1996), 87.
10. Ibid.
11. Ibid., 86.
12. Ibid., 88.

I did not hate my friend. I was angry and disappointed in her. But with all the things I spewed about her as a person, did it sound like love? Had I made her into an enemy? Perhaps she had misunderstood what she had done. Or hadn't known. Did I ever discuss it with her or had I, in a huff, decided it, or she, wasn't worth my time? I still allowed it to pain me. Was I enjoying licking my wounds so much that I actually didn't want to work through it? Still, I felt conflicted, shattered, torn apart. I could barely concentrate on anything else.

I did need to pray for myself. To be whole again. To apologize to God for allowing my state to interrupt our communion. For going overboard from lament into complaint. For drowning out the voice of the Spirit calling me to relinquish the pain. For circling the center like a hungry beast rather than centering down in God's presence. To ask forgiveness as I gave forgiveness.

How had I forgotten what I had marked years before in the first book of Thurman's I had read?

> It is in the climate of quietness, stillness, silence, that we get release from the involvement which keeps us defocused, scattered, entangled. . . .
>
> The Spirit of God, brooding over this stuff of our lives, will knead it and fashion it, infuse it with life, or withdraw vitality from some aspects of it. All of that is the divine prerogative. Our obligation is to make the exposure.[13]

---

13. Howard Thurman, *The Growing Edge* (Richmond, IN: Friends United Press, 1956), 40, 52

I've told people that the only way you can fail at prayer—or meditation—is not to show up for it. I *had* been praying and centering—perhaps more haphazardly of late because of travel and deadlines.

That is where the discipline Lewis talked about comes in. This discipline allowed Lewis not to strike back when condiments were poured on his head at a lunch counter or as a policeman's club crushed his skull. It was the discipline that enabled Lewis, Thurman, and King to write several books, deliver multiple sermons and speeches, travel, teach, lead delegations, and raise families over their careers.

It was the discipline in which Jesus engaged. From the Gospel accounts, he regularly went away alone to pray. It would have been improbable that he spent all night talking. He had to spend a lot of time seeking his Father, opening himself to God, and listening. That time, that discipline, empowered Jesus to forgive his enemies. And the friends who betrayed him.

I thought about my calling. As a person of faith who accompanies others on their spiritual journey, I can't afford to allow myself the luxury of living an undisciplined spiritual life. As someone who lives with a chronic condition, I can relate to what Thurman wrote next.

It is in some ways like the thing that happens when a person has some kind of disease that he has to watch. He knows that he is perfectly normal in many ways; but he must never forget, in all of the details of his living, whatever the nature of his excitement and joy and enthusiasm—he must never forget that his heart isn't quite as strong as it was.[14]

---

14. Ibid.

"Pray for yourself," my spiritual director said.

I better understand what she was saying.

It's at the center of the Lord's Prayer—to pray for myself for forgiveness as I offer forgiveness to someone else.

It's a simultaneous movement that needs to happen over and over again, if I continue to call myself a Christian.

So I've been praying for myself.

Forgive me, Lord. Give me the grace to forgive my friend. Forgive me for fixating on her and the wrong she did. Give me the grace to let it go when I sit in your presence and to leave it with you when I get up. Forgive me for not asking sooner. Give me the grace to walk in forgiveness. Amen.

I think my spiritual director would be pleased.

7

Howard Thurman:
Contemplative and Sacred Activist

JACQUELYN SMITH-CROOKS
AND LERITA COLEMAN BROWN

Behold the miracle! . . . Love loves; this is its nature. This does not mean it is blind, naive, or pretentious, but rather that love holds its object securely in its grasp, calling all that it sees by its true name but surrounding all with a wisdom born both of its passion and its understanding. . . . Such an experience is so fundamental that an individual knows that what is happening to him [or her] can outlast all things without itself being dissipated or lost."
—Howard Thurman, *A Strange Freedom*

An age-old problem in the United States has been propelled once again into the headlines of international media. It has held people almost spellbound in every arena, be it print or other more modern means of technology. The problem: racism/racial supremacy. Appearing in its many forms, the issues of racism and the need to confront it was brought to the forefront, with one of the many questions being: "How will we respond?" Will our response be based on media or meditation?

There is no single or ironclad answer, for they vary—sometimes widely. Some members of the families whose relatives were killed in a Charleston, South Carolina, church quickly said, "We forgive him." Later, other friends and family members spoke out to the contrary. While forgiveness may not be likely for them, they did speak of justice.

A few months earlier, another unarmed African American man was killed by police in Ferguson, Missouri. Almost immediately, there was a vehement response to this act of injustice. These stories are just the beginning of more recent tragedies, injustices, and responses to the public resurrection of bold and blatant acts of racism.

People from faith communities made efforts to intervene about that which was, for all intents and purposes, an unspeakable issue of race and racism. Whether in sacred or secular circles, blatant and bold disregard for the lives of Black men and women warrants a response, one that transcends a reaction.

As African American women who are educators and spiritual directors, we decided to address this point of intersection, not because of recent events but because we recognized much earlier that a response stemming from contemplation has a greater likelihood of moving toward the wisdom that comes through discernment.

There are different schools of thought about where and when a contemplative approach is appropriate and evolves into action. Some people assume that the contemplative is a passive stance that protects one from the risks associated with vulnerability. We are less inclined to see it as passive acceptance or inaction. It is not a risk. It is a "leap of faith" that necessitates listening to the inner and the outer. This leads to the place where the contemplative and justice meet—the intersection. Language and its attending meanings impact interpretations outside of our narrow circles. In this essay, we use *sacred activism* and *the contemplative* interchangeably.

All too often in secular and sacred circles implicit and explicit racism may go unrecognized or unacknowledged. As members of the Spiritual Directors of Color Network, we believe it is of great importance that we incorporate this absence in this essay. Here we speak about the importance of acknowledging the place of the contemplative in addressing issues of social injustice and racial injustice in particular.

The Rev. Dr. Howard Thurman contributed much to the incorporation of the contemplative in social/racial justice efforts. An African American theologian and mystic, Thurman was reared in an African American Baptist Church, served as dean of the chapel at Boston University and Howard University's Andrew Rankin Chapel. He was cofounder of the first intentional, interfaith racially and economically integrated church in the United States—The Fellowship of All Peoples—in San Francisco, California. His association with the renowned Quaker Rufus Jones is believed to have been another influence on his practice of the contemplative and social justice. Not only was he well known for his place in the academy, Howard Thurman served as spiritual advisor to Dr. Martin Luther King Jr. during the civil rights movement of the 1960s, and thus played a critical role as a "behind the scenes" leader in the development of an alternative to violence in the dismantling of racial injustice in America.

Thurman chose to engage in work that would serve all people and to use the contemplative experience as a path to peace, joy, and power. He wrote about this desire—especially for oppressed people—in *Jesus and the Disinherited*.[1] He found it both intriguing and inspirational that Jesus chose to conduct his ministry with oppressed people, the poor and dispossessed like himself, rather than the aristocracy or even middle classes of Jewish and Roman society. *Jesus and the Disinherited* became a cherished favorite of Dr. King and whenever he marched, he carried this classic book.

Thurman had the prophetic ability to make a connection between the silence and scrutiny of one's inner life and the work for social justice. He encouraged Dr. King and other organizers of the Movement to utilize contemplative practices. In particular, Thurman stressed the importance for marchers to examine their inward journeys and to use nonviolent responses to what was often very violent confrontation.

Ever emphasizing the vital role of silent prayer, Thurman circulated meditations and conducted worship so that members could quiet their hearts and hear the messages that Spirit offered them. Among the many meditations he wrote (e.g., *Meditations of the Heart, The Centering Moment*), some specifically addressed social justice issues. Thurman also created other equally moving and relevant spiritual resources (e.g., *Deep Is the Hunger, For the Inward*

---

1. Howard Thurman, *Jesus and the Disinherited* (Boston: Beacon Press, 1999).

Journey, The Creative Encounter) to support the inner growth and strength for the outer work of social justice advocates.

Sacred Activism

Howard Thurman coined the term "sacred activism" after his meeting with Mahatma Gandhi in the early 1930s. It is this same theme that has been echoed in sacred and secular circles with a bit of frequency in more recent years. It is a way of responding from deep within, making a conscious decision to maintain a focus on the inner workings even in the midst of untenable and inhumane circumstances. As the old African American spiritual says, "You can kill my body but not my soul." Spiritual resistance is a soul-filled response to a negative circumstance, whether on the part of an individual or a larger community. "In quiet and confidence is your strength" (Isa. 30:15, AKJV).

The philosophy of sacred activism via internal change and transformation proffered by Dr. Thurman was integral in shaping a social reality and movement that conformed to his understanding of religious knowledge, that spoke both to the innate worth of the disinherited as well as the well-being of the community.[2] Howard Thurman writes: "There is no argument needed for the necessity of taking time out for being alone, for withdrawal, for being quiet without and still within. The sheer physical necessity is

---

2. Luther E. Smith Jr., *The Mystic as Prophet.* (Richmond, IN: Friends United Press, 1991), 107.

urgent because the body and the entire nervous system cry out for the healing waters of silence."[3]

Thurman was described by some critics as a "back bender" of the civil rights movement. Thurman responded by saying that social change has its origin not so much in the public events; it is inextricably linked to a shift that transforms the mind, spirit, and body of the individual. "He rather gently and powerfully moved through the world in a spirit of grace, dignity, and humility."[4]

What happens during that solitary time, that introspective time, the time of contemplation? The movie *Selma* provides a poignant example of what can happen in such a moment. On the Edmund Pettus Bridge, Dr. King's decision to turn around was preceded by a moment of contemplation. Dr. King attuned himself to the spiritual discipline, listening to the inner voice of spiritual discernment. In so doing, Dr. King used a "waiting" moment to make a "weighted" decision. It was a decision that was not embraced by many of those on the march. In the final analysis, it became clearer that his act of contemplation prompted him to make a wise and judicious decision—one that probably protected the marchers from extreme physical harm.

In the stillness, whether it is in silence, the stanzas of a poem or the lyrics of a song, in the personal or collective rhythms and beats of a musical instrument, "God breaks in." Creativity happens, life results, energy is restored, purpose is defined, direction is given, transcendence takes over, and one communes (dwells/abides) with

---

3. Howard Thurman, *Meditations of the Heart* (Boston: Beacon Press, 1981), 27–28.
4. Walter Fluker, quoted in Rich Barlow, "Who Was Howard Thurman?" accessed on November 10, 2015, http://www.bu.edu/today/2011/who-was-howard-thurman/.

God. Barbara Holmes says "contemplation is a spiritual practice that has the potential to heal, instruct, and connect us to the source of our being."[5] It creates a shift in our reality structures.

Making Connections

Jacquelyn

My introduction to the role that activism plays in changing social and economic policies and structures occurred during the civil rights movement of the 1960s. It began in church during my teen years. Of course, the language of activism was not part of the vocabulary that was used in our household, church, or the Macon, Georgia, community in which I was born and raised. Whether a fiery and animated conversation someone had with God publicly or during a more quiet moment of prayer, I came to understand what it meant to make a connection. Later, I acquired new language for these moments. It was the "contemplative."

In my parents' house and the larger community, being a "card-carrying" member of the NAACP was an imperative for Black people. Therefore, my siblings and I were no exception. It was not enough to carry the card, my father made it clear to us that active participation in the youth group was equally important. This meant that as card-carrying members of the youth division, we would also be involved in workshops and trainings for active resistance efforts, i.e., the demonstrations, picketing, sit-ins, and other related

5. Barbara Holmes, *Joy Unspeakable: Contemplative Practices of the Black Church* (Minneapolis: Fortress Press, 2004), 29.

activities. Later I learned that this training had incorporated "contemplative practice" of focusing. Not only was it a matter of being centered, it was also about being faithful and clear about the reason we were willing to take a leap of faith and the possible outcome or other acts of resistance with a counternarrative. As Dr. Martin Luther King Jr. said, "Faith is taking the first step even when you can't see the whole staircase."[6] These acts marked a beginning of the intersection of some of the sacred activism and biblical reference that "faith without works is . . . dead" (James 2:26).

Our willingness to participate in nonviolent acts of resistance could not always be traced to our innate desire to respond in this way. For some, it was more of a desire of "an eye for an eye." In dealing with adversaries, it was understood that one should protect him/herself by fighting back. My brother was one who had stated firmly that he was not going to take the blows without returning them. As important a cause as it was, he was not allowed to participate.

For my sister and me, it was imperative that we learn new ways of responding if we planned to engage in the marches, picketing, and demonstrations. We had to learn a new way of resistance. It emanated from within. Grounded in love, strength, and discipline, we learned to maintain our focus, to "keep our eye on the prize and our hand on the plow."

On Saturday mornings, the youth division of the NAACP provided training for the mind, body, and spirit. During this preparation for engaging in nonviolent resistance during the civil rights protests and public demonstrations, understanding and demonstrating

---

6. Martin Luther King Jr., undated speech.

the sacredness of our participation was an important element. The training included simulations and role-playing designed to offer nonviolent responses to the anticipated confrontations with those seeking to maintain the status quo; i.e., systemic racial injustice in public and/or private spaces.

Not long after the early training, I was put to the test while picketing on Cherry Street in Macon, in front of Peggy Hale, one of the major department stores for women. Our focus was insuring that African American clerks were hired and African American shoppers be allowed to try on clothes before purchasing them. While I was carrying the picket sign, a white man came up to me, pulled phlegm from his chest, and spat directly in my face. However mild this act might appear, I had not expected a frontal attack being "in my face." Nevertheless, I called on some of the simulations from the trainings and recalled lyrics of a few of the songs we had sung many times in church, NAACP, and mass meetings: "Keep Your Hand on the Plow, Hold On," and "Ain't Gonna Let Nobody Turn Me 'Round."

As Thurman reminds us in *Jesus and the Disinherited*, "If a man knows precisely what he can do to you or what epithet he can hurl against you in order to make you lose your temper, your equilibrium, then he can always keep you under subjection."[7] I wiped my face and "kept on a-walking" with my picket sign "as I marched up to freedom land."

A few years after my involvement in the activism of the civil rights movement of the 1960s, I was in a college in Illinois, and I encountered a different kind of racism. It was covert—and what

---

7. Howard Thurman, *Jesus and the Disinherited* (Boston: Beacon Press, 1996), 18.

I came to recognize as psychological warfare: "microaggressions" that really were not "micro." They constitute ingredients for psychological implosion. It was during this stage of my life that I began to feel compelled to make a choice—to choose between the sacred and sanity. I opted for sanity.

I found it almost impossible to maintain my focus on and commitment to that which was sacred. It was easier to disidentify with Christianity and the church, including the socioreligious education and training that I had undergone in both church and the NAACP. So I stopped. I distanced myself except when I felt that it was necessary for family events or funerals.

A number of years later, I "met" Howard Thurman in my search for a theology that offered me a balance I was seeking. It would be one in which the depth of the meaning of "love mercy, do justice" would be truly inclusive of critical consciousness, social action, and the mystical nature of Christian spirituality. I no longer felt that I had to compartmentalize or deny my desire to experience my wholeness and not be a "divided self." Moreover, it was like giving agency to my voice, and acknowledging my identity as an African American woman, who chose to be a Christian, and I was in good company. As I later heard Walter Fluker say in a sermon, "What you are looking for is also looking for you."

When I discovered Thurman, I felt that I had found something special and had arrived at an intersection of the sacred and social justice, especially racial justice. The connection was deepened when I learned that, quiet as it was kept, Howard Thurman was a spiritual advisor to some of the leaders of the civil rights movement, including Dr. King. This man, Howard Thurman, was a preacher and a practitioner, who spoke a language that was truly liberating and offered a way to internalize and seek to live a theology of freedom and justice for all.

So, who was Howard Thurman, and what was it about him that spoke to me? It was the way in which the sacred spoke to social activism, especially racial justice. The insights I continue to gain allowed me to meet Jesus for the "second time." I was at the intersection of faith and action in the presence of Jesus. I had encountered Jesus not in the image of one whose strong gentleness would lead to his martyrdom and great following, but as a role model who did not constrain and restrict and who was a radical revolutionary, liberating from psycho-spiritual, sociopolitical, religious, and other prisons. I could see his work as sacred activism. This was the message delivered to me by Howard Thurman.

Lerita

I grew up in Pasadena, California, in the 1950s and 1960s with the vestiges of social injustice not quite as visible as they were in the South. I remember our father sitting us down as young children to have the "race conversation" as we prepared for a family visit to Arkansas. He explained that things were different "down there," and we would see signs for "Colored" and "White Only" at restrooms, restaurants, and neighborhood pools. Racism in California more subtly reared its ugly head with neighborhood covenants barring Blacks, Latinos, Asians, and sometimes Jews from purchasing homes. I had not yet learned about the loss of homes and livelihoods as Japanese "citizens" were carted off and sent to internment camps during World War II.

My first clear taste of racial injustice occurred as a member of the first wave of Black students desegregating University of California campuses in the early 1970s. Although I attended a legally mandated desegregated high school with Whites, Blacks, Asians, and Latinos, the result of the *Brown vs. Board of Education* decision and subsequent lawsuit, the White students and professors at UC Santa Cruz behaved quite differently than the ones I encountered at John Muir High School. They frequently treated me as if I were an alien from another planet and many believed that I was "let in" as an Equal Opportunity Program (EOP) student at the University. I was very aware that I entered through the regular admissions process and with a California state scholarship.

The university setting, however, provided an opportunity for me to cross paths with Jan Willis, a young assistant professor of religion who was also African American. A budding Tibetan Buddhist scholar, she taught my roommate and me how to meditate.[8] This simple act of cultivating a divine inner connection altered my life forever.

Since that time, I have allowed messages emerging from my contemplative practices of silence and stillness to guide me as I choose to engage the inner and the outer, utilizing a contemplative approach (seeking inwardly) to determine the necessary external action (the outer) to address racial injustice.

I have been most intrigued with Howard Thurman's notion of "inner authority," the idea that each individual has some power over what he or she allows into one's inner sanctum:

---

8. Jan Willis, *Dreaming Me: Black, Baptist, and Buddhist—One Woman's Spiritual Journey* (Somerville, MA: Wisdom Publications, 2008).

There is in every person an inward sea, and in that sea there is an island and on that island there is an altar and standing guard before the altar is the "angel with the flaming sword." Nothing can get by that angel to be placed upon that altar unless it has the mark of your inner authority. Nothing passes "the angel with the flaming sword" to be placed upon your altar unless it be a part of "the fluid area of your consent." This is your crucial link with the Eternal.[9]

I learned that it is vital to exercise some control over how I respond to and internalize the reactions from others, particularly in determining my worth. Connecting with my inner divinity serves as a constant reminder that it is only God who establishes my worth. Contemplation also allows me to "hear" what my proper role is in securing social justice for all. Not everyone is called to march or protest publicly. In fact, Dr. Thurman was highly criticized for not playing a more active public role in the movement. Yet many foot soldiers, many workers served in different capacities in the civil rights movement. Some people opened their homes, cooked meals, and tended to wounded demonstrators. Others prayed, provided legal services, and cared for the children of marchers. Likewise today, Spirit may call us in a variety of ways—perhaps to plan and organize demonstrations, establish and monitor social media sites, write an essay or a letter to the editor, join the Peace Corps, teach, or volunteer. Sometimes it is difficult to discern what our specific role should be. Thurman suggests that by being still and silent, by going within and asking, an answer will emerge. At other moments, just by

---

9. Howard Thurman, *Meditations of the Heart* (Boston, Beacon Press, 1981), 15.

being present, by paying attention to what is apparent, we receive instructions. Yet there are often vital questions to be answered. The first is: "What is the purpose?" Then, "Is my participation making me feel good about myself, or am I truly called to this place at this time?" Finally, "Do I see myself in those who are most oppressed?"

Contemplation as Spiritual Discipline

Thurman would probably take a moment, and then he would respond by saying: "Don't ask what the world needs. Ask what makes you come alive, and go do it. Because what the world needs are people who have come alive."[10] Spiritual disciplines "are meant to 'ready' the mind, the emotions, and the spirit. They are no guarantor of Presence. . . . God reveals His Presence out of the mystery of Being. With all of my passionate endeavor, I cannot command that He obey."[11]

Although Howard Thurman (1899–1981), mystic, theologian, and spiritual adviser did not use the terminology "thin place," the contemplative practices he promoted are exactly what Mark Roberts[12] advocates. Some say that Thurman was a man before his time because he always encouraged people to "center down," embrace quietness, befriend stillness, and cultivate a relationship

---

10. Howard Thurman, personal communication cited in Gil Bailie, *Violence Unveiled: Humanity at the Crossroads* (New York: The Crossroad Publishing Company, 1996), xv.

11. Luther E. Smith Jr., *Howard Thurman: Essential Writings* (New York: Maryknoll, 2006), 45.

12. The Rev. Dr. Mark D. Roberts is the executive director of the Max De Pree Center for Leadership at Fuller Seminary.

with silence. Thurman, a contemplative as a young boy, writes about why silence and stillness are so vital and how they ready the spirit for an encounter with God. He utilized regular silence and stillness to move into what might be described as a "thin space." This idea suggests that we, too, may be able to create these experiences for ourselves and for others in order to access the gifts, the wisdom that often emerges in these instants.

Some would argue that Thurman's significant thin place experience was in India at Kymber Pass, where he received the inspiration to establish the first intentional interracial church, the Fellowship of All Peoples in San Francisco, California. Yet Thurman's constant kindling of his relationship with silence and stillness helped him to apprehend his eternal link with everyone and every living thing and thus ignited a burning desire to break down the racial and social barriers of his time. Thurman's experiences and writings raise the question again: Can embracing silence and stillness create if only temporarily a thin space that inspires each of us to let go of the boundaries, cross the barriers, and experience the connection that we have with each other?

Conclusion

The focus on Howard Thurman is not sheer coincidence. It was very timely. Clearly, he continues to serve as both an unofficial spiritual director for other struggles for civil rights, and he serves as a role model for those who seek ways to move past marginalization and disinheritance. He was on the fringe even in doing what he felt called to do; yet his voice was and continues to be heard throughout the world. Thurman was reminded in his many contemplative moments, and communicates in his sermons and writings, the same truth Jesus taught: that each of us is created by God, is a child of God, and that is what we must always carry in our hearts.

The year 2015 marked the fiftieth anniversary of the beginning of the civil rights movement and Mrs. Rosa Park's conscious decision to "not be moved." The strategies and tactics of nonviolence shared by Howard Thurman continue to be used by some African American college student leaders. In addition to making their voices heard as Black student leaders, these students, their allies, and others in Black Lives Matter movement demonstrations, employed nonviolent strategies and tactics such as hunger strikes, boycotts, nonviolent protests, and prayer.

These efforts had widespread impact throughout the country because of the student leaders' choice to be still and know, to turn inward in order to move forward/go outward (respond to the external). They were able to tap the inner wisdom for answers that offered the possibilities that are found in sacred activism. These answers serve as tools for change and transformation. As a spiritual teacher, Bernard Alvarez reminds us: "Activism without spirituality is an angry mob."[13]

---

13. Bernard Alvarez, "Activism without Spirituality Is Just an Angry Mob," Collectively Conscious, accessed on November 10, 2015, http://collectively conscious.net/memes/bernard-alvarez-activism-without-spirituality-is-just-an -angry-mob/.

8

A Reflection on Contemplation and Social Justice in a Global Era

Jung Eun Sophia Park

In terms of spirituality, and spiritual direction in particular, the relationship between contemplation and social justice is one of the most familiar yet challenging. Nowadays, spirituality is often considered a personal enterprise that just aims toward the integration of one's individual faith. However, spirituality involves, at its best, a communal dimension that emphasizes the interpersonal and social relationship of an individual. Thus, social justice should be an essential part of an individual's spirituality. However, there is no clear definition of the term "social justice"; it is used differently according to particular contexts. This essay will explore theological implications of the concept of social justice in relation to contemplation and examine social justice actions in the context of the global era through the case of Jeju Island in South Korea.

Contemplation and Social Justice

Contemplation is the goal and the fruit of the practice of many spiritual traditions. Contemplation, in certain traditions, is a rarely achieved level of spiritual practice attained only in monasteries. However, more and more people consider contemplation to be a mode of being open to and acting mindfully in everyday situations. I believe that one of the most commonly used definitions of contemplation, "a long, loving look at the real," by the Jesuit priest Walter Burghardht,[1] brought the notion of contemplation into our ordinary and secular world from the transcendental world. In using the word "real" in regard to contemplation, the transcendental dimension of God is included in the imminent one. Through God's eyes, the person contemplating the world brings certain actions out of love and justice.

Regarding the aspect of action of contemplation, *The Merriam Webster Dictionary* gives two meanings for contemplation: 1) The act of thinking deeply about something; and 2) the act of looking carefully at something.[2] These two definitions are fascinatingly interrelated in terms of action, and both include an action component, despite contemplation's seemingly inert and passive appearance. Contemplation and action are often thought of separately, but it is arguably almost impossible not to participate in creative action when one looks at the real in a loving and mindful way. Clearly contemplation should be connected with certain activities that emerge from the action of thinking and looking. Even in the

---

1. Walter J. Burghardt, "Contemplation: A Long Loving Look at the Real," in *An Ignatius Spirituality Reader*, ed. George W. Traub (Chicago: Loyola Press, 2008), 89–98.
2. https://www.merriam-webster.com/dictionary/contemplation

midst of responsible action, a person must be in the process of con-templation. Therefore, how can we appreciate the notion of social justice in the terrain of contemplation?

Social justice, as a fundamental Christian principle, provides a lens through which an individual or a community takes a "long, loving look at the real." The very definition of social justice has long been complex and ambiguous. For some, social justice means serving the poor in a soup kitchen, while for others, social justice is participation in protests against injustice, violence, and oppression. Nevertheless, it is clear that social justice itself is not action. Yet people often understand social justice as an orientation or spiritual principle and contemplation as action.

One of the ways to understand social justice is to see it as dis-tributive justice, which has to do with notions of fairness in the dis-tribution of benefits and burdens in a given society.[3] As a spiritual principle, social justice includes an understanding, analysis, and responsible action, which make for truthful freedom, the meeting of needs, and the promotion of law.[4] However, in promoting the law, tension and conflict sometimes arise in obeying the law. In many cases, the notion of social justice supersedes the obedience of the law and leads into a creative reaction according to the law of love, which emerges from the spirit of contemplation.

In the principle of social justice, the value of equality or fair-ness indicates that every human being should have dignity and

---

3. Loretta Capeheart and Dragan Milovanovic, *Social Justice: Theories, Issues, and Movements* (Brunswick, NJ: Rutgers University Press, 2009), 29.
4. Nicholars Sagovsky, *Christian Tradition and the Practice of Justice* (London: Society for Promoting Christian Knowledge, 2008), 214.

their basic human needs should be satisfied by the community. In Christian teaching, particularly in Catholic social teaching, human dignity and solidarity are emphasized. The Christian notion of social justice comes from the Messianic vision, which inaugurates the kingdom of God *here and now*. Additionally, a deep sense of solidarity with other human beings prompts people to act for the common good. For example, Thomas Merton, an activist Cistercian monk, felt invited to social justice action when he had a contemplative moment of solidarity, what he called the "Louisville Epiphany":

> In Louisville, at the corner of Fourth and Walnut, in the center of the shopping district, I was suddenly overwhelmed with the realization that I loved all these people, that they were mine and I theirs, that we could not be alien to one another even though we were total strangers. It was like waking from a dream of separateness, of spurious self-isolation in a special world.[5]

In deep awareness of being connected with others, the notion of social justice begins and solidarity functions as a ground for any social action.

Contemplation and Social Justice Action

Social justice action finds its root in contemplation, which is not an enclosure, but rather openness to the world; it is not separation

---

5. Thomas Merton, *Conjectures of a Guilty Bystander* (New York: Doubleday, 1989), 158.

but rather solidarity. Thus, it is fair to say that sheer contemplation should lead one into some voluntary action or participation in transforming the society and the whole world.

Personally, I believe that participation in any social action emerging from moral obligation is beautiful, but in particular, an action rooted in deep contemplation is more powerful because it exists beyond emotion or sheer speculation, though not excluding them. Thus, we can say that contemplation should guide a sincere seeker into social action for justice in the world.

However, social justice action could also lead a person into contemplation. Contemplation could begin at a rally for peace and justice, or it could be time spent serving food at a homeless shelter. Any social justice action is an invitation to contemplation, not because the person becomes holier or more valuable, but because through the action, the person faces oneself, including one's own fear, anger, and frustration. Without contemplation, an action can be an emotional reaction and can make one easily frustrated. More importantly, this contemplative moment in the midst of social justice action leads one to the deep and loving gaze of God, which is given to the person, to all people, and to the entire world.

Activism and revolutionary zeal ideally involve the spirit of contemplation. Action for social justice should invite one to a level of contemplation and underscore the importance of prayerfulness and mindfulness. The relationship between contemplation and social justice actions are like a Mobius strip, with one side inseparable from the other.

Social Justice in the Global Era

In this global era, there have been challenges to reframe the notion of social justice, which had been dominant in Western society during the twentieth century. After World War II, various threads related to sociopolitical and economic realities were woven into the discourse of social justice. In the ensuing dialogue, the voices of minorities in terms of gender, race, and power were located at the center. For example, women's rights regarding internalized and externalized oppression gained greater importance in the justice discourse. Racial injustice against African Americans resulted in the civil rights movement in the United States. Finally, the injustice that indigenous or colonized people have suffered have also gained greater attention.

Now, many people challenge the notion of social justice because its scope of understanding has been limited in the Western world. In this era run by neocapitalism, the concern for social justice should be expanded to a global scale. Scholars such as Olaf Cramme and Patrick Diamond argue that globalization has profoundly affected "how we think about social justice and the extent to which we believe it is attainable."[6] In this context, social justice is no longer related to one nation or a single community, but is instead deeply related to multiple nations, operating beyond national borders.

Poverty, or the misdistribution of wealth, is a primary injustice in this global context and creates a serious concern. In the Global South, people suffer from abject poverty and lack of resources,

---

6. Olaf Cramme and Patrick Diamond, eds., *Social Justice in the Global Age* (Cambridge: Polity Press, 2009), 3.

while the Global North enjoys material abundance. At the same time, even in wealthy societies, the disparity between the poor and the rich is expanding, and younger generations, who have fewer economic, social, or cultural resources, suffer from debt and job insecurity. Furthermore, the global and local situations are intrinsically interrelated, so social justice must consider both.

Another area of concern for social justice is the phenomenon of multiculturalism, which is a result of immigration. Distinctions in culture can be expressed through language, religion, food, family structure, and lifestyle. Like other new experiences, multiculturalism has created both challenges and opportunities within societies. In particular, the experience of immigrants tends to be repeated by old racist notions expressed in new ways.[7] For example, immigrants from Muslim cultures experience discrimination in the form of Islamophobia.

New immigrants also suffer from inequality among themselves, a situation often based in education and economic status. For example, high tech professionals from around the world who live in the Silicon Valley enjoy ample resources, while other immigrants who flee from war as refugees have difficulty finding places that welcome them.

Yet another challenging area of social justice in the global era is ecology. Unlike the discourse of social justice, which is primarily limited to human society, ecological social justice includes any life such as plants, animals, and even the earth itself. In other words,

---

7. Loretta Capehart and Dragan Milovanovic, "Multiculturalism, Globalism, and Challenges to Developing Forms of Justice," *Social Justice*, 77.

environmental justice indicates the connection between the distribution of resources among peoples and the relationship between humans and the rest of the natural world. Ecological justice would link environmental concerns with social justice regarding race, class, and gender.[8] Pope Francis's encyclical *Laudato Si'* claims that climate change has brought misery to the poor because only the rich have the capability to defend themselves against natural disasters.[9] In examining the ways in which we distribute justice, we see that ecological concern is the most challenging area of social justice in our global era, and as such, we must emphasize the need for ecological conversion.

Global corporations invest capital in places where labor is cheap and natural resources are available. Ecological justice includes problems of water, food, air pollution, and climate change, but the distribution of the resulting harm or burden is difficult to measure appropriately. Often, the capitalistic or free market system assumes control over the entire global market, so that the use of capital in injustice remains problematic.

Very often, ecological concerns and multiculturalism are related through sociopolitical and economic forces, so that many people who desire justice feel powerless and frustrated. I believe this is the place where contemplation and spirituality can take a significant role. How can we regain a strong sense of human solidarity or a spirit of interconnectedness? If we belong to the group that has less power or benefits, how can we stand against the destructive power?

8. Ibid., 94.
9. Francis, *Laudate Si'* (Vatican City: Literia Editrice Vaticanan, May 24, 2015).

I do not have answers to these challenging questions, but the contemplative spirit or contemplation—which emphasizes a long and loving gaze at any given situation—must give direction to people in order to give more creative and life-giving responses.

An Ecological Justice Struggle on Jeju Island

In spiritual direction, we sometimes encounter enormous levels of anger, frustration, and fear stemming from the realization that we do not have solutions for injustice. We face difficulties and experience a flux of emotions and thoughts. Although we lack clear-cut resolutions, we are invited to hold apocalyptic hope in the midst of our frustration.

Let me share an example of a contemplative response to an ecological concern. I visited Jeju Island in Korea several times between 2010 and 2014 for my field research on shamanism. Jeju is a volcanic island famed for its natural beauty and for its spirituality, which is very much women-centered. Geographically, Jeju Island is a fairly marginal site off the Korean mainland; it is also an entry port from other countries such as Japan, Taiwan, and China. Because of this geopolitical location, Jeju can be understood as a borderland.

Recently, the town of Gangjeong has become a central place on the island where various groups of people gather, constructing a community together to make an effort toward ecojustice and peace. The location of Jeju Island—from a military perspective—is ideal for defending East Asia's Pacific naval power; controlling China; and aligning with Okinawa, Taiwan, Guam, and Hawaii. However, because of ecological destruction threatened by the construction of a naval base, many peace activists from all over the world have gathered together on Jeju. The construction plan was announced in 2008; since then, people concerned for the ecology of Jeju Island have been protesting this plan.

Gangjeong has become a symbolic site where global and local concerns intersect. Because the construction plans involve the destruction of rocks that are distinct and a crucial part of the beauty of the island, many people from across Korea began to gather and protest the construction of the camp.

Out of these conflicts, the Jeju islanders were split between those who support the construction plan and those who do not. This plan also raised interest among many real estate investors so that the price of land became high. As such, native islanders can no longer purchase it. As has happened in many other places, this has resulted in native people losing their land and becoming poor laborers.

Yet in this struggle, through its long years, activists have become residents of the island. Native Jeju residents have also proposed the peace movement called Pax Asiana, which promotes collaboration with other Asian countries, rather than being initiated by one strong country, to seek eco-justice and nonviolence.[10]

In my research, I experienced many people collaborating toward the goal of peace on the island. The Catholic Church of the Jeju Diocese has established a faith community where two priests reside permanently and peacefully on the island, to rally against the

---

10. Seongjoon Ko, Keunhyung Kang, Dongsuk Chang, Donghyeun Chung, Kyeonghee Kim, *East Asia and Jeju, the Island of Peace* (Jeju: Jeju National University Press, 2004), 43.

construction. In addition to the priests, some religious women have also volunteered to live there and join this peace movement. Every day on the street, these activists offer Mass and prayer, and various groups of people gather from beyond the island to participate in dancing and artwork as acts of resistance. Presently, the naval base and a residential complex for the families of naval officers have been constructed. However, the long-term struggle for eco-justice continues.

In a recent spiritual conversation with a young activist, I found that her social activism action had already brought change into her life. This woman moved to Jeju five years ago and has since been promoting eco-justice there. She is currently enrolled in graduate school, but has already decided to live her life as an activist as a resident on Jeju Island. When I asked her what motivated her to live on the island, she replied, "I heard that dolphins which reside in the Jeju Sea are almost extinct because of the navy camp construction and so came to visit here. Then, I found that I could not leave."[11]

Gangjeong has become a site where people from around the globe stand together in peaceful protests every day. After daily Mass, people stand on the street together, singing and dancing. The activists who have come with various concerns, such as the peace movement, an antimilitary stance, animal rights advocates, and natural environmental advocates, create a community that shares a central concern against the construction of the naval base at Gangjeong; they call themselves the "Gangjeong Keepers." At the street Mass on Christmas Eve, the people celebrated joy and peace and shared their desire to continue this peace movement together.

---

11. Pink dolphin Hwang Hyoung Jin, interview with author, December 25, 2015.

Social justice is often hard to discern and human action seems powerless before the strong power of capitalism with its imperialistic and militant force. However, in creating a community working for peace and celebrating the Eucharist, human effort continues in an apocalyptic hope.

Closing Remarks

In a neoliberal, free market economy, those who are poor and suffering from injustice become more invisible and voiceless. In our global era, local and global concerns intersect and cause tensions and conflicts, while those most affected continue to suffer. We need to regain a contemplative spirit. I believe that if we contemplate the world through the lens of social justice, we will hear a deepened groan from nature, including our global and local neighbors, and we can be creative amid an overwhelmingly frustrating situation. Only in the spirit of contemplation can we face frustration, disappointment, and fear. Then, and only then, can we envision an apocalyptic hope.

9

Religious Intolerance and Gender Inequality

Ruqaiyah Nabe

As an interspiritual, interfaith, and multifaith spiritual director, I pondered the topics of contemplation and social justice
and the contrast or link between the two. How do they connect, if
indeed, they do? One dictionary definition offers: "To contemplate
is to look at or view with continued attention or observe thoughtfully; to consider thoroughly; to think fully or deeply about, and to
have as a purpose or a plan; religious contemplation."[1] Religious
contemplation? Strangely interesting. When I pondered the word
"contemplation," one of my first thoughts was of the prophets or
founders of the three Abrahamic faiths of Judaism, Christianity,
and Islam. Each of these men—Abraham, then Moses of the Jews;
Jesus, the Christ of the Christians; and Prophet Muhammad
(pbuh) of the Muslims (may peace be upon them all)—withdrew
from their communities from time to time to find a place in
which they could abide in silence. Moses went to Mount Sinai

---

1. http://www.dictionary.com/browse/contemplate

and received the Ten Commandments (Exod. 34:28–29); Jesus went to lonely places (or *the wilderness*) to pray (Luke 5:16); and Muhammad (pbuh) used to go in seclusion in the cave of Hira, where he received the Holy Qur'an (Qur'an 96:1). Even Siddhartha Gautama, the Buddha, sat beneath the Bodhi tree to receive the Eightfold Path to Enlightenment.

These holy seekers used their time in silence to go within, to pray, meditate, commune with their Creator and Universal Mind—and to contemplate. One might imagine that they used these periods of silence to observe the "worlds" in which they lived; to receive answers to questions and solutions to problems that served their communities. These answers and solutions ultimately became the faith traditions, spiritual practices, and ways of life that we know today. No doubt these historical figures were observing the uncompassionate ways in which humans were behaving toward each other, and trying to find ways by which all of our ancestors could be better inhabitants on this earthly plane. Answers to the aforementioned question—why contemplation and social justice—began to unfold.

The topic of social justice, in and of itself, seems fairly clear. Everyone deserves fair and equal treatment—to be treated justly. One scholar says it this way:

> Social justice is defined as . . . promoting a just society by challenging injustice and valuing diversity. It exists when all people share a common humanity and therefore have a right to equitable support for their human rights, and a fair allocation of community resources. In conditions of social justice, people are not discriminated against, constrained,

or prejudiced on the basis of sexuality, religion, political affiliations, age, race, belief, disability, location, social class, socioeconomic circumstances, or other characteristics of background or group membership.[2]

There are myriad issues that fall under the subject of social justice, among them: civil rights, income disparity, employment opportunity, unequal education, poor housing, domestic violence, and human trafficking/slavery.

Spiritual direction is a ministry that serves seekers of "divine truth"—seekers of the holy, so to speak—people who are searching for ways to establish or strengthen their connection with a Force, a Power, or Source they believe to be greater than themselves. This may be called by many names, or no name, be it Allah, Ahura Mazda, Creator, Elohim, God, Great Spirit, Jehovah, Jesus, or Universal Mind. Some seekers may be atheists, agnostics, Gnostics, humanists, naturalists, or naturists who have spiritual practices but are not devotees to any organized religion. Some may draw from more than one religion or spiritual practice, calling themselves interfaith or interspiritual. There is a place in the ministry of spiritual direction for everyone.

Spiritual directors who serve in interfaith, interspiritual capacities serve seekers of faiths and spiritual practices that may be different from their own. The objective is to keep an open mind and,

---

2. Matthew Robinson, "What is Social Justice?," Department of Government and Justice Studies, Appalachian State University, http://gjs.appstate.edu/social -justice-and-human-rights/What-social-justice, accessed June 28, 2014.

most importantly, a heart that is open and spacious to all directees who seek their service.

One obvious benefit of contemplative practice is the opportunity to pause and think. Taking time out of our activities of daily living to slow down and sit in silence for a short while provides the opportunity to take a few deep breaths, slow the pulse, and decrease the stress in our busy, hectic lives. It provides time to quiet the "chattering monkeys," clear the clutter, and it opens our minds. Clarity of mind leaves space to find answers to questions and solutions to problems. It offers the possibility to see from a different perspective. Sitting in silence, meditation mode, and prayerful contemplation opens the heart and renders it more spacious.

As a Muslim, the ignorance, misconstrued ideas, and discrimination against Islam are of particular concern to me. Muslims are viewed as misogynists, murderers, and terrorists, and its women are perceived as victims. Islam is viewed as a violent religion instead of the peaceful religion that it was and is meant to be. The attacks of some few individuals do not bode well for the image of the Islamic community. Clearly, I, nor most peace-loving Muslims, do not applaud or condone such atrocious and heinous acts of violence committed in the name of Allah and Islam. Persons who commit these acts are considered extremists. They are no different from the Ku Klux Klan (KKK), who consider themselves Christians. While growing up in America, I do not recall ever hearing the words "terrorism" or "terrorist" used to describe the KKK. I do remember that the KKK used the cross, the most holy and sacred symbol of Christianity, a *burning* cross, to terrorize America's Black citizens. Does the average Christian American—Black, Caucasian, or otherwise—behave as the KKK do, condone what they do, or wish to be associated with them? I don't think so. I certainly hope not. In like manner, good, loving, peaceful Muslims do not wish to be associated with or want to be judged by the actions of extremists—nor should they. There are good and bad people in *every* group and sadly, in every religion. Further, the "jihad," the holy war, is not meant to kill people indiscriminately. It certainly is not meant to kill innocent people. It does not mean to behave aggressively but to defend oneself from the aggressor who intends physical harm upon you—as in *any* war involving combat. However, the greater jihad refers to the struggle within—the challenge to overcome temptation to go off course, ignore one's religion, and not submit to the will of God (Allah). That *is* what Islam means—*submission.* It behooves those who are not Muslim to learn something about Islam before judging all Muslims in the same way.

As for women in Islam, I am an American woman of African descent who was reared in a Christian family. I embraced Islam in my late teens. It is quite common for me to be asked, "Why would you, as a woman, choose a religion such as Islam?" The answer to that question would probably require a separate essay. However, I feel no need to defend my choice or the religion. I do feel the need to exchange, share, and examine differences, as well as similarities; i.e., to educate those who know little or nothing about the faith. The following, in reference to women, is a popular saying among Muslims. The well-known scholar Shaikh Adram Nadwi says:

Women have a special place in Islam and are honored. When she is a DAUGHTER, she opens the door of Jannah

(Paradise) for her father. When she is a WIFE, she completes half the Deen (Faith) for her husband. When she is a MOTHER, Jannah (Paradise) lies under her feet. If everyone knew the true status of women in Islam, even the men would want to be women.[3]

For those who hold misconstrued notions about Islam, especially about women in Islam, I remind them (Muslim and non-Muslim, women and men) that it was Khadijah, the first wife of Muhammad (pbuh), who was the first person aside from the Prophet (pbuh) to embrace Islam. She was a Christian. She was a wealthy widow, and she financed Islam in its early stages. She was a business woman, and she was the young Muhammad's employer. Her proposal of marriage to him set the precedent for women to propose to men.

The Prophet's (pbuh) youngest wife, Aishah, was a scholar, and men, the companions of the Prophet (pbuh), consulted with her regarding the Hadith (the actions and sayings of the Prophet [pbuh]), many of which she wrote.[4]

During his days of prophecy, Muhammad (pbuh) appointed at least one woman a leader (Imamah or Shaykha), Um Waraqa, in charge of her dar (community) of mixed genders.[5] A number of the Prophet's (pbuh) wives were women he married after his twenty-five years of marriage to Khadijah and *after* her death—women,

---

3. Shaikh Akran Nadwi is from Jaipur, India. He is an Islamic scholar, a graduate of Oxford University, a research fellow, author, and teacher.
4. Karen Armstrong, *Muhammad: A Prophet for Our Times* (New York: HarperCollins, 2006), 223, 228.
5. Amina Wadud, *Inside the Gender Jihad* (Oxford, England: Oneworld Publications, 2006), 156.

most of whom were widows following the loss of their husbands due to war and who were maintained as part of the community, some of whom were leaders in their own right.[6]

A number of the women in the Prophet's (pbuh) household, including his daughters, were scribes.[7] There are numerous other examples of women in Islam who held positions of leadership and honor.

Mistreatment of women did not begin with Islam. It goes without saying that it is not the religion, but the interpretation of it—by and for men. Observe the Old Testament of the Holy Bible regarding the stoning of women who supposedly brought shame on their father's houses.

> But if this thing be true and tokens of virginity are not found for the damsel: then they shall bring out the damsel to the door of her father's house and the men of the city shall stone her with stones that she die because she hath wrought folly in Israel to play the whore in her father's house, so shall thou put away evil from among you. (Deut. 22:20–22)[8]

Merlin Stone, author of *When God Was a Woman*, referred to this particular section of the Bible when she explained, "Once the Hebrews wiped out earlier customs, it was time to put their politics

---

6. Armstrong, *Muḥammad*, 87.
7. Brian Arthur Brown, *Forensic Scriptures: Critical Analysis of Scripture and What the Quran Reveals About the Bible* (Eugene, OR: Cascade Books, 2009), 123.
8. The Holy Bible containing The Old and New Testaments, Revised Standard Version, translated from the Original Tongues, being the Version set forth A.D. 1611, revised A.D. 1881–1885 and A.D. 1901. Compared with the most ancient authorities.

into practice. The Levite priests set forth laws for the Israelites from the time of Moses, which demanded virginity until marriage for all women. Once married, only the wife had to adhere to total fidelity. If either law was broken, the punishment was death by stoning or burning. Non-compliance or deviation was sin, punishable by a disgraceful and excruciating death sentence."[9] Stone also mentions that "Jezebel was murdered in the most gruesome manner, described in morbid detail in the Bible. She was used as an example and a warning to any disobeying or potential disobeying women."[10]

Scripture, all scripture, be it the Hebrew Scriptures, the Gospels and New Testament, or the Holy Qur'an, is subject to interpretation or application to justify circumstances benefiting the one who is using it. Muslim men who use the Holy Qur'an to subjugate women, espoused in the doctrines of the faiths that preceded Islam, use it the way in which some Caucasians use the Holy Bible to justify enslavement of Blacks. Women, Muslim and non-Muslim, who are subjugated to second-class citizenship and abuse by virtue of the misuse of religion, can also use Scripture to justify their fight for fair and equal treatment and freedom to control their lives. They too can use the chapters and verses of the sacred texts to authorize, back up, defend, and document their argument.

A number of Muslims argue that Prophet Muhammad (pbuh) promoted women's rights. Ranya Idliby, a Palestinian, said that "he was a champion of women's rights,"[11] and Shaykh Jamal Rahman,

---

9. Merlin Stone, *When God Was a Woman* (Dorchester: Dorset Press, 1990), 190.
10. Ibid., 188.
11. Ranya Idliby, Suzanne Oliver, and Priscilla Warner, *The Faith Club: A Muslim, A Christian, and A Jew—Three Women Search for Understanding* (New York: Free Press, 2006), 114.

a Suni, Sufi spiritual director from Bangladesh, hails the Prophet (pbuh) "a radical feminist of his time centuries before the term was coined."[12] Shaykh Jamal Rahman also says that "it is necessary for the Muslim community to return to the sacred values of the Quran and the teaching of the Prophet Muhammad 'so that man might incline with love towards woman.'"[13]

Let us take a look at women in the United States and around the world: About three hundred years ago, early European Christian settlers conducted the Salem Witch Trials in Massachusetts. While some men, called warlocks, were executed, it was mostly women who were put to death based on accusations of practicing witch-craft. Twenty people were executed between June and September 1692, the majority of them women.[14]

The suffragette or women's rights movement took place from 1848 to 1920.[15] One of the major rights women fought for was the right to vote. The women's liberation movement surfaced in the late 1960s and was active into the 1990s. There were three waves of campaigns and protests during these periods.

The first wave addressed legal obstacles to gender equality, including voting and property rights, sexuality, family, workplace,

---

12. Jamal Rahman, Kathleen Schmitt, and Ann Holmes Redding, *Out of Darkness into Light: Spiritual Guidance in the Quran with Reflections from Christian and Jewish Sources* (New York: Morehouse Publishing, 2009), 69.

13. Qur'an 7:189.

14. Jess Blumberg, *A Brief History of the Salem Witch Trials,* October 23, 2007, http://www.smithsonianmag.com/history/a -brief-history-of-the-salem-witch-trials -175162489/. See also http://womenshistory.about.com/od/salempeople/tp/Victims -of-the-Salem-Witch-Trials.htm.

15. "The Women's Rights Movement, 1848 to 1920," U.S. House of Representatives: History, Arts, & Archives, http://history.house.gov/Exhibitions-and-Publications /WIC/Historical-Essays/No-Lady/Womens-Rights/

and reproductive rights. There was also a push for gains in professional status, military, media, and sports inclusion. The second wave (ending in the 1980s) covered domestic violence, marital rape, custody battles, and divorce law. Rape crisis and battered women's shelters emerged. The third wave, in the 1990s, included additional issues of sexuality. Protests against pornography were ushered in.

In the second millennium, not the Middle Ages or three hundred years ago, women are still dealing with issues such as date rape, campus rape, military rape, human trafficking, and murder. Women have been fighting for comparable job positions and equal pay for equal work for centuries. America has yet to elect a female president in its 239-year history. When asked about the rights of women in Islam, Imam Feisal Abdul Rauf responds with the reminder that Muslim nations have elected women heads of state in some of the most populated Islamic countries. He, in turn, poses the question: "Could one agree then that the United States lags behind the Muslim world in granting equal rights to women—and that the reason America has never had a female president is because of its Judeo-Christian ethic?"[16]

Clearly, we have an issue of gender inequality in "the land of the free and the home of the brave"—"America, the beautiful." It is sad that it exists here and sad that the focus is away from Americans and pointed at "the other." Yet the problems of inequality, misogyny, oppression, and violence are not exclusive to the United States. A women's movement, the Women's Social and Political Union

---

16. Imam Feisal Abdul Rauf, *What's Right with Islam: A New Version for Muslims and the West* (New York: HarperCollins Publications, 2004), 217.

(WSPU), existed in Great Britain in the late nineteenth and early twentieth centuries. Women in New Zealand received the right to vote in 1893. In South Australia, women achieved the right to stand for Parliament in 1895, and women in Canada (except Quebec) received the right to vote in 1919.

While the women's liberation movement was emerging in the United States in the 1960s and 1970s, it was also surfacing in other developing countries and spreading throughout the Western world into a worldwide movement—Europe, parts of Asia, Turkey, and Israel.

When I was in China in 1984 on a transcultural nursing tour, our group witnessed billboards throughout Beijing informing the public that it was okay to have baby girls. This campaign existed because baby girls were still the victims of infanticide in the rural areas of China. The one-child rule had been instituted in the 1970s. Because boys were valued more than girls, baby girls were detected with the use of amniocentesis, and female embryos and fetuses were aborted. China lifted its one-child rule in 2015. For one reason, China realized its surplus of boys and young men, which, no doubt, is causing national problems.[17] Maybe now baby girls will have a chance.

There was the tragedy that took place when a Taliban member shot a young Pakistani girl, Malala, in the face because he believed that girls should not attend school that cannot go without mention.

---

17. Didi Kirsten Tatlow, "Not Enough Women in China? Let Men Share a Wife, an Economist Suggests," Sinosphere (blog), New York Times, October 26, 2015, https://sinosphere.blogs.nytimes.com/2015/10/26/china-polyandry-gender-ratio-bachelors

His extreme act of violence still has Muslims wondering how he arrived at his belief and action. Today, Malala is seen as a guest on TV promoting her cause for availability of education for all girls. She won a Nobel Peace Prize for her bravery.

It is evident that women in the United States, the Western world, and the world at large have many issues in common—gender inequality and, unfortunately, crimes of violence committed against them. It is also evident that these problems are not confined to any one religious group, race, or nation. It is global. Solutions must be sought at home and abroad. No one group or nation can afford to point the finger at the other, or to exist in denial. Women and girls are as valuable as men and boys, and they deserve to be perceived in this way. They deserve to be treated with dignity, honor, and respect within their families, communities, society, and the world. In the final analysis, true freedom cannot exist for one group if the other group is held in bondage. No individual, community, or nation can truly prosper if any other is held in bondage. Its equilibrium will be off-kilter. The surplus of boys in China resulting from the discarding of baby girls is an example.

The problems that jeopardize women's rights need not only be reduced, they need to be eradicated. Here in the United States women can continue the struggle by banding together to support each other. Stand up, be seen, and speak out. Frederick Douglas once said, "Agitate!" In 1964 Senator Margaret Chase Smith ran for president, followed in 1972 by Congresswoman Shirley Chisholm. Both women undoubtedly knew that they had little chance of being taken seriously, but they took a stand. That was decades ago. In the 2016 election, the country finally gave serious consideration to electing a qualified woman to the position of president of the United States. Women can build upon the acts of these brave women and the gains achieved through the women's movements. We stand on their shoulders!

Rights gained must be strengthened, and laws passed must be enforced. Hold rallies, petition government officials, and do not support or vote for politicians who do not support women's causes or promote improvement in their basic human, civil, and equal rights. Lobby to introduce new and improved laws so that violators are appropriately penalized and rehabilitated. Demand that public servants such as law enforcement officers are more vigilant and diligent in carrying out their pledge to serve and protect. Continue the fight for equal pay for equal work. Young girls and young women can fight for their rights and follow the lead of Malala, who continues the fight for all girls to have a right to education. Clergy must be part of the education process to positive change. They must be brought to the table for dialogue, and sermons must address the issue of domestic violence. Scholars and theologians of all faiths need to educate the community and lay clergy who follow Scripture literally without examination and deliver content by fear tactics and judgment.

If indeed the United States is a nation that governs according to "separation of church and state," then politicians need to act accordingly—practice their own religious doctrines and beliefs without infringing upon the personal and religious rights of others who believe differently from them:

The First Amendment (Amendment 1) to the United States Constitution prohibits the making of any law respecting an establishment of religion . . . impeding the free exercise of religion. . . . Congress shall make no law respecting an establishment of religion, or prohibiting the free exercise thereof.[18]

The United States should, by all means, continue espousing its policies and procedures of democracy and rule of law, but it must be carried out "with liberty and justice for all" races, religions, and human beings—male and female.

Women have to continue to compete for leadership positions in the workplace, the religious setting, and the political arena. They must give serious consideration to backing up and supporting female candidates for president and other key political positions, not only because they are women who can champion their causes, but because they are qualified to do the job. Women should not promote or elect any politician who is not interested in their concerns. If America really practices what it preaches, it can really set an example for the rest of the world.

In her book *Healing the Soul of America*, Marianne Williamson states:

---

18. Amendment 1 Freedom of Religion, Speech, Press, Assembly, and Petition. Passed by Congress September 25, 1789. Ratified December 15, 1791. The first 10 amendments from the Bill of Rights. "Congress shall make no law respecting an establishment of religion, or prohibiting the free press exercise thereof, or abridging the freedom of speech, or of the press, or the right of the people peaceably to assemble and to petition the Government for a redress of grievances." Source: https://constitutioncenter.org/interactive-constitution/amendments

Our nation, for many reasons, has developed a public personality that has great difficulty admitting when we have been wrong. Politicians, who ideally should be our primary healers, seem particularly loath to offend any voters by pointing out America's errors. This deeply obstructs our national healing because a collective, like an individual, simply cannot grow without taking responsibility for its own mistakes.

This clearly annoys other nations, which find our sometimes constant finger-wagging in their direction while refusing to admit our own transgressions the stuff of outrageous nerve.[19]

America and the world need healing from its problems concerning religious intolerance and gender inequality. Williamson's thinking brings us back full circle. It brings contemplation and social justice into full focus, respectively:

"Contemplation is to observe thoughtfully; to consider thoroughly."

"Social justice . . . it exists when all people share a common humanity."

Contemplation is not exclusive to founders of religion, clergy, or spiritual directors. If equal rights and social justice are to exist for all human beings, public servants, law enforcement officers, government officials, and politicians will need to raise their level of consciousness, emotional intelligence, sensitivity, and compassion.

---

19. Marianne Williamson, *Healing the Soul of America: Reclaiming Our Voices as Spiritual Citizens* (New York: Touchstone, 2000), 90.

They need to become more involved in the utilization of spiritual tools. The practice of contemplation serves as a good starting point as decisions made by individuals in these positions impact the lives of the citizens they are appointed and elected to serve, protect, lead, and represent. Secular laws that are introduced, passed, and applied with conscious, thoughtful consideration for the good of all involved would create a nation that is in balance with spiritual laws—"Do unto others as you would have them do unto you," and "Love thy neighbor as thyself."

The behavior of individuals in positions of public trust, along with those of us who count ourselves more "ordinary" citizens, can, through contemplation and action, increase in sensitivity, compassion, and fairness. These changes then can begin to correct and eradicate social injustices and crimes against humanity for all—regardless of race, national origin, ethnicity, religion, or gender. Care for the well-being of every human being is that which will produce the Great Society that President Lyndon Baines Johnson spoke of—an equal and just society.

10

Multifaith Conversation as a Tool for Spiritual Empowerment

LESLIE SCHOTZ

We are spirits having a bodily experience" is the gist of what I have heard from kindred spirit colleagues. The expression sounds innocent enough. It reminds us that we did not choose to be born and our dying is not something we can prevent. It is our time on earth that gives our lives meaning.

Yet we live in a world where people suffer at the hands of other people. That suffering cannot necessarily be compartmentalized into "body, mind, or soul." We are whole beings who respond as one unit. In the Jewish religion, part of our liturgy is the *Sh'ma*. It is Hebrew for the word "listen." In the *Sh'ma*, we are called to listen to God with all our hearts, souls, and might. Yet the prayer is in the singular form. "You shall love the LORD your God with all your heart, and with all your soul, and with all your might" (Deut. 6:5).

The word for prayer in the Hebrew language is *l'hitpalel*, which is a reflexive verb meaning that "you do prayer to yourself." Praying is a transformative action that has the potential to change or perhaps refine one's very essence. We can find the answers to our deepest challenges within ourselves by making room for God to dwell there.

I had the great privilege to be ordained as a spiritual director through the Jewish Renewal movement founded by Rabbi Zalman Schachter-Shalomi, of blessed memory, who was known affectionately by those who loved and respected him as "Reb Zalman," My class was the last spiritual direction class he witnessed become ordained as spiritual directors, as he died before the following class was ordained. I myself had only met Reb Zalman twice in my life. The second time I met him he gave me a special blessing to teach spiritual direction for children.

In my education as a spiritual director, or in Hebrew *mashpi'ah*, my teachers referred to spiritual direction as "holy listening." I was encouraged to pursue a doctorate in spiritual direction through the first woman to lead a rabbinical seminary, The Academy for Jewish Religion, located now in Yonkers, New York. Rabbi Dr. Shoshana Weiner, who paved the way for higher study in the field of interfaith studies, started the spiritual direction program at Aleph: the alliance for Jewish Renewal.

Leviticus 19:18 in Hebrew is *V'ahavta l'reyacha kamocha*, which has been translated to mean "love your neighbor as yourself." Many teachers have taught that a difference between Christianity and Judaism is that love defines Christianity and justice defines Judaism. Yet I would like to propose an intersection rather than a parallelism to this simplistic definition. If the Jewish definition of love is connected to justice and the Christian concept of love is connected to charity, we can still see an essential commonality.

In Hebrew, *Tzedek, tzedek tirdof* means "Justice, justice you shall pursue." The Hebrew root word for "justice" is also related to the word for "charity" in Hebrew. *Tzedek* means justice. *Tzedekah* is the term for sharing wealth, giving to those who are in need of food, clothing, shelter, or a job. Edward Kessler, the founder and executive director of the Centre for Jewish Christian Relations in Cambridge, writes about "The Jewish Concept of Justice."[1] In his conclusion, he brings attention to the United Nations Universal Declaration of Rights exemplifying four features of the Jewish understanding of justice. They are: the dignity of each human being, the equality of each human being, human responsibilities, and freedom.

While at SUNY at Stony Brook, one of my fields of interest was Africana Studies. Professor Amiri Baraka, once known as Leroi Jones, encouraged me to find my roots as a Jewish woman. Later, I would learn while reading *How I Became Hettie Jones* by Baraka's former wife that he was the father of a black Jewish daughter. As I studied *The Negro* by W. E. B. DuBois,[2] I remember one of those "aha!" moments with Professor Baraka. It had to do with who is black and who is white.

Professor Baraka posed a question to the class regarding identity and skin color. He asked how we determine who is black and who is white. He said that there were Italians who were darker in

---

1. Edward Kessler, "The Jewish Concept of Justice," *The Way*, Supplement 97 (2000): 69–78, http://www.theway.org.uk/back/s097Kessler.pdf.
2. W. E. B. DuBois, *The Negro* (New York: Henry Holt and Co., 1915).

skin tone than certain black folk. Then he pointed out hair. That was something I could deeply identify with: as a girl growing up with curly, kinky, frizzy hair, I had always felt different.

Growing up in an all-white town, I had felt poisoned by racism and anti-Semitism. I was brought up to believe that we are all one, yet the reality exemplified in the public schools I attended was clear. You must be white and Christian to be accepted. I learned how to hide being Jewish. I passed as white. I was the beneficiary of white privilege as long as I straightened my hair and hid my truth, my Torah, my journey.

Now it is time to heal from the poison of racism, anti-Semitism, anti-Muslim sentiment, anti-Christian violence, and all the hurts that human beings inflict upon one another. We are each called to be Holy Listeners. We live in a multifaith world. Reb Zalman coined the term "Deep Ecumenism": all the spiritual, religious paths lead to the same place.

In the project for my dissertation, I integrated a lesson in the supplemental Hebrew School focusing upon Black History Month. In a nonjudgmental space I allowed a student's racism to surface so that we could learn how to replace the ignorance with diversity and respect. Much to the benefit of the students, this school's teaching staff represented diversity in and of itself. As a Jew, I consider myself a woman of color. Although my parents checked off the "white" box on my birth certificate, I never mark "white" on forms about race. I create a box that says Jewish and check it off. Israel is right next to Africa. We are closely related. The two teachers teaching with me were an Asian Jew and a Jamaican Jew. Certainly we cannot always tell who is who by how people appear to us. It is up to those of us who do not necessarily appear to be "of color" to educate those whose racism springs up in unexpected and expected places. That is what I am called to do as an embodied spirit contemplating social justice.

In Yiddish the term for dirt is *shmutz*. It is time to stop sweeping the *shmutz* under the rug and heal ourselves spiritually so that repair of the soul can lead to a repair of the planet. In Hebrew, the term for repairing the soul is *tikkun hanefesh*. The way to say repairing the world is *tikkun haolam*, or *tikkun olam*.

One of the highpoints of my ministry as a rabbi and president of the Bay Shore Interfaith Clergy was to be the first female rabbi to speak in the local mosque. This was deeply profound for me on a number of levels. As a woman, a Jew, and a rabbi, I felt my action helped to embody social justice. One of my rabbinical teachers said the most important thing a rabbi can do is just show up. As each human being is created in God's image, when we show up we bring God with us.

Here is some of what I said on that occasion:

Minister and Professor Jamal Rahman explains that it is important to discern judgment in the choice of a spiritual guide. He emphasizes the point in the following story.

> *Such is the case of the hidden teacher in the story about two famous sheikhs who arrived ostentatiously at a local mosque to prepare to pray. One sheikh took his shoes*

off and carried them with him as he stepped outside the mosque. The other teacher carefully placed his shoes outside.

After prayers, the sheikhs, whose every movement had been watched with intense interest, were asked to explain their actions. The first sheikh said that he took his shoes inside with him so that no one would be tempted to steal them, thus saving that person from a wrongdoing. The other said that by keeping his shoes outside he gave some-one the opportunity to resist temptation to steal and thus gain merit in heaven.

"How wise and how noble," the townsfolk agreed among themselves. To get a better understanding, they went to a sage and asked which of the sheikhs was the "true" teacher.

"Neither," replied the sage. "While you all were busy watching and judging, and the two sheikhs were engaged in their calculation of saving and gracing, none of you noticed a poor, shoeless man with a heart of gold who stepped into the mosque with reverence, prayed with deep fervor and devotion, and beseeched Allah to bless every-one. He is the real sheikh. His heart is turned in devotion to God, and he simply brings to the moment a heart that can respond to God."

Minister and Professor Rahman says that the presence of such a guide in one's life is a blessing. As it says it the Quran 50:33, "This kind of teacher conforms to the descriptions of an evolved being: One who is 'humble before the Unseen and brings a heart that can respond.'"[3]

As an embodied spirit, connecting within one's own tradition while reaching out to that which connects us all is the challenge of balance.

Social justice requires the ability to communicate effectively in the art form of understanding facts tempered with compassionate perspective. The ability to socialize means that we must determine how to tell our stories and listen for the essence of what matters to those we meet. We must decide what we can share, what can be understood, and how to connect our experiences into reference points of wisdom for our friends and neighbors. Every introduction is a potential friend. The challenge is in the conversation: what to say, what not to say, whether verbally or nonverbally. Is speaking necessary or is listening presence required for the situation? Discernment is a tool for effective communication.

My own spiritual practice is to walk outside in nature. Psalm 100 in Hebrew is *Ivdu et Hashem b'simcha*. Serve God with joy. Experiencing the creation of God connects me to the Creator. In Hebrew, the unpronounceable word for God includes the Hebrew root word for "being." That root word is a verb, meaning that God is an action. Just as the word for praying is a reflexive

---

3. Talk at Masjid Darul Quran: The Muslim Center of Long Island, Bay Shore, New York, was November 19, 2012, quoted in Jamal Rahman, Kathleen Schmitt, and Ann Holmes Redding, *Out of Darkness into Light: Spiritual Guidance in the Quran with Reflections from Christian and Jewish Sources* (New York: Morehouse Publishing, 2009), 6.

action, God too is not stagnant. God is active. God was. God is. God will be.

In our highly technological world, we realize that the simple truths are healing. Take a breath. Relax. Be in the moment. These are things a baby knows. The baby is completely focused on his or her needs. We sometimes forget to be there for ourselves, the vehicles that connect us to God. It's like trying to run a car without gas. We need to refuel ourselves. Sometimes we need a spiritual friend, guide, or director to be present to our truth, to make a place for God to dwell.

In many Jewish and Christian houses of worship, there has been a decline of children in religious education. Children are hungering for a moral compass. Our news reports have been inundated with the pain and suffering of children by children through unimaginable violence. More than ever it is children who need spiritual guidance.

As I researched spiritual direction for children as part of my own dissertation process, I was most surprised to find lessons about contemplation in resources for public school teachers. At a Spiritual Directors International Conference in New Mexico, it seemed that the contemplative lessons of the Eastern religions such as Buddhism have influenced Christian and Jewish houses of worship. The religion of our parents' and grandparents' generations is shifting into a new paradigm.

In the Torah, which is the portion of the Jewish bible composed of the five books of Moses, we learn that God confounded people's language into pure babbling when the Tower of Babel was built. The people were filled with arrogance in believing that they could reach a God in heaven through physical means. Real spiritual journeying takes emotional grounding. Now is the time for us to learn how to speak each other's languages in order to understand and live in peace with each other's spiritual truths. Together we can balance our lives and learn how to support one another.

Let us pray together and make room for God to join us with love, healing, blessings, mutual respect, and joy. Halleluyah. Praise God.

11

Spend Time with Others: Prepare Your Heart for Social Justice

MAISIE SPARKS

*"If you love only those who love you, what reward is there for that? . . .
If you are kind only to your friends, how are you different from anyone
else?"*

—Matt. 5:46–47, NLT

*"But I entered their world and tried to experience things from their
point of view. I've become just about every sort of servant. . . . I didn't
just want to talk about it; I wanted to be in on it!"*

—1 Cor. 9:22–23, The Message

*"I only saw what I was afraid of. I never saw that you were my
brother."*

—Gerry Bertier, defensive lineman, T.C. Williams
High School (*Remember the Titans*)

It's probably highly sacrilegious to include lines from a
Hollywood movie character alongside the sacred words of
Jesus Christ and the apostle Paul, but while I was watching TV,

eating breakfast, and pondering what I'd do with my day, it just seemed fitting. *Remember the Titans,* a modern-day film classic, stopped my channel surfing as I tried to replace the snap, crackle, and pop of cereal that was quickly becoming soggy and silent. The film dramatizes the 1970s when integration came to a Virginia high school and, more specifically, its football team. Typical of the era, no one was happy with the government-imposed new way of life, and everyone blatantly expressed their hateful attitudes. Although I'd seen the movie more times than I care to admit, this morning I was watching with new eyes and listening with new ears. In addition to the scripted lines I'd heard before, I also was remembering some insightful words from a college lecture: "The 'Other' is always beneficial to us," my professor said, "God is always good. But what prevents us from loving the 'Other' is fear." What I was watching on my television screen was stark evidence of that sad truth. Not only do we live in fear of the "Other," we also live in fear of *others.* The cure, the wise professor offered, was a radical openness to the "Other."

That thought made me put down my spoon, pick up my journal and pen, and ponder what would happen if each of us made it a spiritual practice to spend time with people who are different from us. What would happen in our communities, our nation, and our world if we got to know others beyond the color of their skin, the inscription over their houses of worship, or the label on their handbag? Could "getting to know you" be more than the lyrics of a song? Could those words in action be the antidote to the misery, tragedy, and violence that frightens us all? Is part of our growth as human beings the ability to embrace people who don't look, think, or believe as we do? Perhaps radical openness to others is the key to saving ourselves from hate crimes, inequities, and even world wars. What if we saw in every person a radical invitation to love sent to us by the "Other" himself—or herself—depending on just how radical you want to be.

Separate and Equal

From the first time an infant realizes that its mother's breast is not its own, human beings begin to understand that they are different and separate from those around them. While this understanding is necessary for healthy social and emotional growth, it takes a dangerous twist if we define "other" in a negative way to give ourselves a positive identity. This happens when "other" is interpreted to mean "less than" because of race, geographic location, economic status, religion, or one of the many other ways we like to divvy up humanity. The real tragedy here is that thinking of one's self as superior to others is an inferior thought. It creates suffering for those seen as inferior and phobias in those holding such an illusion. That's been the disastrous reality of "othering" throughout much of human history: destinies of whole groups of people have been derailed because one group thought another group was inferior, threatening, or not even human at all.

America's 240-year history is replete with episodes of the dehumanizing of one group by another. Every time ethnic groups came to this land on a ship, boat, or on foot, they were relegated to plantations, barrios, ghettos, detention camps, and the south side of the tracks. Even the people who were indigenous to this land of the free and home of the brave were marched across the country to be restricted to reservations. It seems that fallen humanity's default position is to see others' differences as making them inferior, threatening, or not even human at all. What's worse is when we see others as existing on the outskirts of God's love.

Bricks, Barriers, and the Bible

God once chose a people, not because they were the greatest, but because they were the least among all nations. He delivered them from making bricks without straw and gave them a good land where they built a temple to honor him. Eventually for many worshippers, ritual practices in the temple ceased to reflect the wholehearted devotion owed to the liberating God, especially the commandment to love one another and to show that love in action. As Jesus Christ walked around Jerusalem, he was moved to reformulate Jeremiah's prophetic warning (7:9-11) against approaching the Holy One as if truly penitent while harboring the intention to continue transgressing. When Jesus saw what was happening in his Father's house, he took care of business. He drove out those he saw taking advantage of the poor and undermining the sacred intentions of temple worship. This is the most outraged Jesus ever appears within the Gospel stories. Why? Because he saw many who were "othered," didn't have open access to the most holy, divine "Other." So what did Jesus do? On the cross, he tore down the curtain that separated the "Other" from mankind; no one needed permission from anyone else to have access to the "Other."

Christ: The Consummate "Other"

Fixing our eyes on the "Other" is a good way to get a right perspective on "othering." One thing that's interesting about the time and place in which Jesus lived was its cultural diversity. Jewish, Roman, and Greek cultures made up the melting pot called Jerusalem at that time, and Jesus had to engage with them. Born of Jewish parents, he had to know his religious heritage. Growing up under Roman rule, he had to respect its financial and tax system. Influenced by a Grecian understanding of commerce, trade, and politics, he surrounded himself with businessmen and women who could navigate and support the fledgling new way of life that would arise after his death, burial, and resurrection. In this multicultural environment, with all its racial prejudices, economic disparities, and cultural differences, Jesus, a being who was totally "Other," emptied himself of himself and joined the diversity called humanity. As the Gospel of John records, the Word (Other) became flesh (other) and dwelt among humanity. God in Christ didn't hold on to his "otherliness," but let it go so that he could live and learn and love his creation. I have experienced "letting go" as one of the most difficult spiritual disciplines to practice. Most of us hold on to things, attitudes, and ideologies long after they're served their usefulness. Sadly, that includes our biases, both conscious and unconscious.

From the outset, God knew that humanity feared the new, the different, the "other," so the first thing the angel Gabriel said to Mary, the mother of the "Other," is, "Do not be afraid." This mysterious Other/other that she was to carry had to be received as a gift so that it could be given in the same way. This Other/other, a mysteriously holy one, was to have a life totally dedicated to others. Jesus's sermon one Sabbath revealed just how dedicated he was to others, especially those who were thought to be less than other others.[1] He was to preach the Good News to the poor, heal the brokenhearted, set at liberty those who were bound, give sight to the blind, and liberate the oppressed: a great vision statement for just about any social justice ministry. But the disruption of imperial order by such a vision was so other, so different, so selfless, the Roman authorities couldn't tolerate his luminous call to fulfill the biblical mandate to love one another without measure, and so they killed the Other/other. Since he really was like no other, he did the unthinkable, the unimaginable, the totally unbelievable, and resurrected himself from the grave. Not only that, but after being seen by many people for forty days, he left earth and left a message that was to be shared with those in Jerusalem, Judea, Samaria, and the uttermost parts of the world. The message was this: the Good News of relationship with the "Other" was for all people.

The book of Acts records that on the day of Pentecost, the followers of this Other/other who were meeting in an upper room were brought into contact with devoted Jews from every nation: Parthians, Medes, Elamites, and dwellers of Mesopotamia, Judea, Cappadocia, Pontus, Asia, Phrygia, Pamphylia, Egypt, parts of Libya, and visitors from Rome, both Jews and proselytes, Cretans, and Arabs (Acts 2:9–11). This diverse group heard the Good News about the Other/other proclaimed in their own language. How ironic, since language had separated people since the Tower

---

1. Luke 4:18

of Babel forced us to reach out to one another across the barrier of varied languages. Now, not even language would keep us apart from the "Other" and others.

A few years ago, I experienced a small victory over the language barrier. I had the opportunity to be part of a mission trip to St. Petersburg, Russia. I had known that I would be experiencing a different group of people and language when I first said yes to the trip, but I was surprised by the fear that gripped me from the moment I landed at the airport. The first thing that hit me was that I couldn't read anything. No words looked familiar. Street signs held no meaning. Independent by nature, I realized that I wasn't going to be able to go anywhere by myself because I wouldn't be able to communicate with others. This fear was causing me so much anxiety that by the second day, I wanted to return home. By then, it was time for our first church meeting. Even though we would have an interpreter, I went with fear of these people and their unfamiliar language. To my surprise, I was greeted with hugs, kisses, and a delicious meal. When they sang "How Great Thou Art" in Russian, I cried tears of joy and relief. I was home; I was in communion with God and newfound brothers and sisters in Christ! Love trumped fear (1 John 4:18). That is always God's intent.

"Others" Are Our Brothers and Sisters

From its earliest days, Christianity sought to embrace the full diversity of people drawn to its tenets. New believers were to be new creatures, people whose most important identity was their relationship with Christ, not their nationality. Everyone was to be welcomed at Christ's table. This Good News was to be shared throughout the known world. The apostle Philip preached it to an Ethiopian eunuch, and the gospel was taken to Africa. The apostle Peter went to the house of a Gentile army officer and realized that the gospel was not just for Jews but that "God shows no partiality, but in every nation anyone who fears him and does what is right is acceptable to him" (Acts 10:34–35). The Apostle Paul had a blinding introduction to the Other/other on the road to Damascus and journeyed to Galatia and Cyprus, Macedonia, Achaia and Greece, Asia, to Greece again and finally to Caesarea, Crete, Malta, and Rome, sharing the gospel to any and all who would listen.

Paul's focus on others was so unlike any other apostle that he deserves a paragraph all his own. A devout and highly educated Jewish leader, Paul, formerly known as Saul, terrorized followers of Christ. The newly forming body of Christ feared him. One believer, Ananias, following a prompting from God, went to Saul, called him brother, laid his hands on him, and watched God remove the scales from his eyes (Acts 9:18). Before we get a Paul, there must be an Ananias who is willing to risk all to save his enemy. There's no miracle like the miracle of enemies becoming friends . . . like those who are far away from each other drawing close. Once Paul realized that others were his brothers, he sought out every opportunity he could to speak to those of other religious traditions, ethnicities, and academic background. He stayed in the home of a Gentile female textile worker, Lydia. He taught at the school of a Greek philosopher, Tyrannus, and he mentored a half breed, Timothy. What is insightful is Paul's rationale for such a strong orientation to others. His reasoning is recorded in 1 Corinthians 9:22–23 and it's two-fold.

First, he wanted others to know the "Other." He also realized that by introducing others to the "Other," he would come to know the "Other" better. As Christ is shared, he also is more deeply embedded in the heart of the sharer. This is the paradox of evangelism. As we give Christ, we receive him more deeply. This transformation often occurs as we live near those who are other to us.

Living with others hasn't been easy. History is replete with crusades, inquisitions, witch hunts, and enslavements—all in the name of religion. Read any world history book, and you'll see that, over the centuries, many people experienced the light of the gospel as fiery heat that burned down their towns, their families, and their future. Yet, despite all this violence, there were individuals who knew there was a more excellent way. Some ministers of the gospel sought to keep cultural respect part of sharing the gospel. Bartoleme De Las Casas was an early challenger to the conquest paradigm of church mission. In 1514, he opposed the enslavement of local people in Latin America and insisted that their human rights be honored and that their introduction to Christ be by gentle persuasion.[2] In Asia, Jesuit missionaries accommodated themselves to the local cultures, mastering Mandarin, Chinese classical literature, and adopting the dress of Buddhist monks.[3] They became respected Chinese scholars. Another Jesuit missionary, Alexandre de Rhodes, traveled to modern-day Vietnam. He empowered indigenous religious leadership and developed local Vietnamese catechists.[4]

---

2. Richard R. Gaillardetz, *Ecclesiology for a Global Church: A People Called and Sent* (Maryknoll, NY: Orbis Books, 2008), 43.
3. Ibid., 44.
4. Ibid., 45.

So what happened? Specifically, in America, the world's "melting pot," why can't we all just get along? Why can't we hold lightly our own primary culture and identify with folks not like us? Perhaps it's because we don't even know folks who aren't like us? To quote Rev. Dr. Martin Luther King Jr., "Eleven o'clock on Sunday morning is the one of the most segregated hours, if not the most segregated hour, in Christian America."[5] He said that back in the 1960s, and nearly sixty years later it's still true. I can only imagine that Christ is still praying his high priestly prayer, "that they may be one as We are one" (John 17:21, Phillips). We are the answer to Jesus's prayer when we can say with personal conviction, "There is neither Jew nor Greek, there is neither slave nor free, there is neither male nor female; for you are all one in Christ Jesus" (Gal. 3:28, NKJV)

Walk across the Room

A tale is told about a young preacher who received a call to an old established church in his city. Six months into his assignment, he was already tired of looking out into the congregation every Sunday morning and seeing the same people sitting in the same place. The Johnson family was always seated front row, north side. The Millers sat six rows back, first balcony center; and the Smiths were always near the right exit door so they could leave the moment the benediction amen was uttered. He'd met every one of them; they were

---

5. Rev. Dr. Martin Luther King Jr., Meet the Press, April 17, 1960, https://www.youtube.com/watch?v=1q881g1L_d8.

all fine families, yet they didn't know each other and the gifts they had to offer one another.

Initially, the young pastor started to get depressed by the sameness of things, but soon it became the inspiration for a sermon he called "Walk across the Room." He didn't quite have a biblical text for his message one particular Sunday morning; his only hope was that his humble invitation would make a big difference. So, as he ended his discourse, he challenged the congregation with these words, "So, if you've been sitting in the same place for more than six months, next Sunday, I want you to walk across the room and sit somewhere else." The room became quieter than it already had been. No one affirmed his idea. There wasn't a clap or "Amen" to be heard anywhere. But the next Sunday, the pastor's words came to life. Some parishioners had forgotten the sermon from the previous Sunday, but enough remembered—including the Johnsons who had been sitting in the same place for three generations—that they walked across the room, sat in new seats, and made new relationships with the people around them. In fact, the Johnsons met the Millers who had come down from the balcony! Different and exciting things started to happen in that congregation because people took the risk to walk across the room.

Recently, a rabbi invited a group of us from an evangelical Protestant congregation to a Sabbath service at his synagogue. In my heart, I immediately accepted the invitation. My spiritual journey has carried me into all kinds of religious gatherings. As I've traveled, I've discovered a host of fellow pilgrims who thirst for the living God. What would this Jewish Sabbath service want to teach me?

I entered the synagogue and was pleased that others from my home church were already there. What's ironic is that I gravitated toward these evangelicals even though I really hadn't gotten to know any of them all that well over the past year that we've been worshipping together. They are white and I am black, and although we sit in the same sanctuary, worshipping the same "Other," there was little that we knew about each other. Tonight, we were both out of our element, and they were glad to see me, and I was glad to see them. I sat with one woman with whom I had spoken a few times; we had started to build a friendship. We whispered that we were enjoying the music, even though it was sung in Hebrew. We didn't know that we should have picked up a prayer book before we entered the sanctuary so we peered over the shoulders of others around us, straining to read a little of the English that would give us some understanding of what was being sung. Finally, the rabbi came up and his teaching was about being inclusive. Being exclusive, he contrasted, is to humiliate others; it's like spilling their blood or murdering them. What's worse than being exclusive is watching it happen and doing nothing about it. When we allow exclusivity, we lose our divinely human form. So, he ended, we're to move from "us and them" to "we are one." Do you think he knew I was writing this reflection? Perhaps the "Other" told him? Whatever the case, the message affirmed and has informed my writing. What's more, the rabbi's teaching supports the writings of Richard Gaillardetz, a Catholic theologian, who wrote that "God's love is neither divisive nor oppressive but gathers up genuine difference in an inclusive wholeness."[6]

---

6. Gaillardetz, *Ecclesiology for a Global Church*, 35.

When I told my niece, Anne, that I was writing an article about spending time with others, she wrote to me in the fall of 2015 with her "Walk across the Room" story that was first written in her class paper. A multicultural course she was taking for her master's degree required students to identify a group of people that they had a prejudice against or were unfamiliar with and spend some time with them. After a little time of reflection, my niece, an open, welcoming person, realized that she had a lot of "prejudgments" about Muslim women. So she started doing some research to find the nearest mosque, only to discover it was just two miles from her home. After contacting the mosque, she attended several of its services and developed friendships with two Muslim women. The experience was nothing less than transformative. She writes:

Before this experience, I believed that all Muslim women were a repressed group, held down by domineering fathers, husbands, and male leaders. Forced to be covered from head to toe, I thought Muslim women were relegated to live in obscurity while men were in charge. In reality, I observed a wide range of personalities and dispositions among Muslim women. One of my new relationships was with a Muslim woman who was a divorced mother of two and a full-time student. The other woman was married, a mother of one child, and worked part time as a medical doctor. One of the most enlightening moments in my experience with these two women was to realize that many of my assumptions about Muslim women actually came from cultural practices, not their religion. Many characteristics attributed to

Islam are more often reflections of a culture I knew little about. Understanding culture's impact on religion was particularly instructive for me. It made me look at America's cultural influences on Christianity. This started some reflection around my own faith and beliefs. I felt embarrassed that my opinion about Muslim women had been formed by many inaccurate assumptions.

How did my niece move from prejudgment to relationship? The same way any of us can . . . by overcoming fear and ignorance and walking across the room. I wonder what would happen if next Sabbath or Sunday a group of Baptists went to a Presbyterian church? Pentecostals attended a Catholic mass? A rabbi and his family worshipped at an Islamic mosque? Or white folks didn't start selling their homes because a black family moved on the block? How can we care about the plight of others if we don't know them as brother and sister?

Lots of folks have looked at our daily "us and them" tension to offer us some ways to understand how we can walk across the room. Milton Bennett, an intercultural communication professor, crafted the "Developmental Model of Intercultural Sensitivity" and suggested that for any of us to gain a sensitivity to and respect for the cultural perspectives of another group, we must move across a continuum from ethnocentrism to ethnorelativism.[7] Simply put, he said that the way you've been socialized isn't the only way to live. Your culture isn't the only culture, and there are many fine ways to

---

7. Dan Sheffield, "Assessing Intercultural Sensitivity in Mission Candidates and Personnel," *Evangelical Missions Quarterly* 43, no. 1 (January 2007): 3.

live a contented life. To come to this kind of understanding, however, you and I have to take a walk from denial and defensiveness and minimization of other people's cultures, to acceptance, adaption, and integration. Getting there will mean experiencing another culture and reflecting on that experience. Both the experience and reflection are needed, for without the reflection, the integration rarely happens. There it is! Contemplation will change the world. We all need time for silent reflection before we speak or act, especially if our words or actions will hurt or harm others.

John Francis Burke, who formed and chaired a multicultural relations committee at St. Jerome's Church in Houston, Texas, wrote of his church's challenge with building a more unified congregation from among its English, Spanish, and Vietnamese constituents.[8] He recounted that his church claimed to be one Church, when it was three or more parallel parishes functioning physically at the same place. His church was like many big American cities with their Chinatowns, Greek towns, Little Italy villages, and "South Sides" where black people live. We visit each other's restaurants, but rarely each other's homes. How do we move beyond that? For Burke, the answer was an intentional effort to respect, honor, and invite the gifts of all communities to the table. Some ways they did that were by praying and singing in all three languages at all meetings. Though meetings were conducted in English, if the primary language of anyone attending was Spanish or Vietnamese, translations were provided, if possible. Domination of meeting time by

---

8. John Francis Burke, "Fostering 'Unity in Diversity': A Case Study of Church Multicultural Relations Committee," *Journal of Pastoral Theology* 6 (Summer 1996): 71–91.

the majority group or personalities was minimized by having the chairperson decide who had the floor, by limiting interruptions, and by making sure that everyone who wished to speak had the opportunity to do so. The goal was not to simply tolerate each other, but for each person to see positive engagement with other cultures as a means of enriching one's own faith. To put it more strongly, the church decided that it couldn't be content with diverse cultures simply coexisting. The universal invitation of Christ demands that diverse cultures engage one another in conversation and social and liturgical interaction. This is the challenge: you have to have all kinds of folks in your church at every level of ministry to be an authentic church.

While that is easier said than done, the alternative, the way things currently are, isn't working. So all I'm saying is to give love a try by walking across the room. What if your courage to do so helped to dismantle prejudices that have kept communities, churches, and countries apart; create theological reflections that arise from the best thoughts of diverse cultures; or develop cross-cultural ministerial formation programs?

Back to the Movie

As I watched *Remember the Titans*, it occurred to me that perhaps what today's church needs is more leaders like Herman Boone, the coach who was given the nearly impossible mission of turning a black team and a white team into a unified team. To achieve his vision, he took the two groups away from their everyday environment. He made them room with a player from a different culture. He forced them to ask each other questions about their families, their preferences, and their future. It was a struggle. Neither side wanted to distance itself from its own understandings and cultural mores. So he turned up the heat, making them practice football and learn about each other until the pain of staying the same became greater than the pain of changing. The two sides saw that it was to their benefit to no longer tolerate each other, but, instead, they decided to embrace each other. Because the two groups finally came to a point where they could celebrate each other, when defensive lineman Gerry Bertier had a car accident that left him paralyzed, the white team didn't show up. Neither did the black team. Only the team showed up. The words that Bertier uttered could have been said by any team member now: "I only saw what I was afraid of. I never saw that you were my brother."

A few years back, I entered a master's program at a Catholic university. Earlier on in my spiritual journey, I would have never considered the thought. I grew up believing that Catholics were going to hell first. Somewhere in my upbringing, I picked up the idea that there was nothing to learn from them and that to spend too much time in their company could lead to the abandonment of all that is good and true. While it is true that they have some doctrinal positions that I can't seem to wrap my brain around, and I often can't find a biblical basis for some of their beliefs (the epicenter of reality for my faith tradition), my life has been enriched by learning with them and about them.

Some of my most joyous memories in recent years have been times spent in their company. I no longer see them as "other," but as fellow pilgrims on this walk with God. I now know more about how God interacts with humanity and how humanity can interact with each other than I ever could have imagined. I've traversed that continuum from denial, to integration, to love. My journey has now prepared me to do the work of social justice. I'm no longer just concerned about the education of my children, but of all children. When a child's body washes up on a shore because his family is trying to flee persecution, that's my child. Jesus still loves the little children; so must we. Red and yellow, black and white, we are all precious in his sight. It's no longer us and them. We're all on this planet together, and we need to make life work for everyone, regardless of race, creed, or color. Would I desire everyone to be Christian? Yes, and I need to live in a way that the deeds I do in God's name glorify and point folks to him. However, in my desire to share God with the others, I must keep in mind that God gives everyone a choice. It's his will that we have a free will and we get to choose what we believe about God. What we don't have is the right to make others "other" if they don't quite see God as we do. Life as it is intended to be requires each of us—Christian, Jew, Muslim, and all religious stripes—to build bridges, not barriers. True religion, whatever the brand, prays and works for Love to prevail. If the world is to have a future, we must all do justice, love mercy, and walk humbly across the room with our God (Micah 6:8).

Should humanity be able to bring peace on earth before the Prince of Peace returns, every heart would have to embrace these words from Sister Elizabeth A. Johnson, a Roman Catholic theologian: "Those who are confident in their faith are not threatened but enlarged by the different ways of others. As we discover a deeper truth than what we thought we possessed as a monopoly, the dignity of difference becomes a source of blessing."[9] I pray that we might all come to see that time spent with others is time well spent. We are gifts given to each other by the most totally "Other" of us all.

---

9. Elizabeth A. Johnson, *Quest for the Living God: Mapping Frontiers in the Theology of God* (New York: Continuum, 2007), 179.

12

A *Sankofa* Moment: Exploring a Genealogy of Justice

Maurice J. Nutt

"Where justice is denied, where poverty is enforced, where ignorance prevails, and where any one class is made to feel that society is an organized conspiracy to oppress, rob, and degrade them, neither persons nor property will be safe."

—Frederick Douglass, speech, April 1886

"I always looked upon the acts of racist exclusion, or insult, as pitiable, for the other person. I never absorbed that. I always thought that there was something deficient about such people."

—Toni Morrison

"You are growing into consciousness, and my wish for you is that you feel no need to constrict yourself to make other people comfortable."

—Ta-Nehisi Coates, *Between the World and Me*

I've always had the uncanny ability to remember. My mind is able to capture and hold the images of people, places, events, names, situations, and occurrences that some might deem unimportant or insignificant. This ability has been useful to fill in the proverbial "blanks" of family stories—both fact and fiction. Some family members thought it odd that I store up in my memory bank what others would readily consider mundane or unnecessary trivia. You see, I found that being inquisitive and asking the seemingly annoying questions of our family elders important because they were the *griots*, the precious keepers of our collective ancestral story. I loved to sit around the "old folks" and listen to the stories about the "good ole days" even if all the stories were not always so good. Even though I may not have clearly realized or understood what I was doing by simply listening, asking questions, and remembering, I was building a bridge back to the past that would help me and my family move forward into the future.

That going back was a poignant and powerful *Sankofa* moment—to go back and fetch that which was forgotten. The word *Sankofa*, deriving from West Africa and King Adinkra and the Akan tribe, is visually and symbolically expressed as a mythic bird that flies forward while looking backward with an egg (symbolizing the future) in its mouth. Literally translated it means "it is not taboo to go back and fetch what you forgot." The concept of *Sankofa* teaches us that we *must* go back to our roots in order to move forward. That is, we should reach back and gather the best of what our past has to teach us so that we can achieve our full potential as we move forward. Whatever we have lost, forgotten, forgone, or been stripped of can be reclaimed, revived, preserved, and perpetuated.

One of my cousins, knowing that I cherished our family's history and genealogy, brought me some old family photo albums. As I pondered the people, places, and occasions displayed in the photographs, I felt transported back into time. In my mind, I relived the events depicted in the picture. There was one picture in particular that captured my attention: it was a picture of me at the age of five paying a visit on Mother's Day, 1967, to my nursing home-bound maternal grandmother, Hattie Ann Britton Duvall. As I looked at me somewhat distanced from my grandmother sitting in the wheelchair, I remembered the pensive feeling I had that day. I was terrified of my grandmother because she was blind from glaucoma. I disliked how she would touch my face to see how I had grown. She would comment to my mother, her daughter, "Bea, you need to stop letting this boy eat too much, his cheeks are getting too fat." I remember my mother forcing me to take a picture with this unknown woman who was my grandmother, and I had feelings of unease and uncertainty. That picture would be the one and only picture that I ever had with my maternal grandmother. In fact, while I never forgot the picture being taken, it was the first time in nearly fifty years that I had seen it!

Today, this picture, which remains in my possession, causes feelings of guilt and shame because I did not know that this blind elderly woman pictured with me was a woman who fought for justice and equality for black people throughout her life. There were no more pictures with my grandmother because less than a year later she would pass away at the age of eighty-two years old. This woman who saw nothing in her later years had witnessed with her once beautiful gray-green eyes a nation marred by racism, injustice, and bigotry.

My guilt in my childish fear and blatant indifference concerning my grandmother stems from learning later in life what a remarkable and courageous woman she was. Hattie Ann Britton was born on September 12, 1886, in Cape Girardeau, Missouri, a relatively small town in southeastern Missouri on the banks of the Mississippi River. Hattie was born shortly after the time of Reconstruction in the United States. Her father and mother were born in Pennsylvania and Ohio respectively and were not born into slavery. However, Missouri was a former slave state and had much of the racial tension common in southern states. Hattie had a sister and a brother. Her mother was a wife and homemaker. Her father was fortunate to have a government job that afforded his family to live comfortably. Hattie had a thirst for education and expressed a desire to attend college. She enrolled in Western University in the Quindaro section of Kansas City, Kansas. Western University (1865–1943) was a historically black university, a Freedman's college established after the Civil War. At the time, it was the only institution for higher learning for African Americans west of the Mississippi River.

After receiving her bachelor of arts degree in education, my grandmother dedicated her life to teaching poor black children in one-room schoolhouses throughout southeastern Missouri. My grandmother stressed that education was the pathway out of ignorance, poverty, and oppression. She was determined to assist children of her race to change the trajectory of their life. It was while teaching in St. Mary's, Missouri, that she met and eventually married my grandfather, Edward Louis Duvall. My grandmother had relatives living in East St. Louis, Illinois, so she and my grandfather moved there to make a living. The couple had eight children: five sons and three daughters.

East St. Louis was the scene of one of the bloodiest race riots in the twentieth century. Racial tensions began to increase when 470 African American workers were hired to replace white workers who had gone on strike against the Aluminum Ore Company. On July 2, 1917, men, women, and children were beaten and shot to death. Around six o' clock that evening, white mobs began to set fire to the homes of black residents. Residents had to choose between burning alive in their homes or running out of the burning houses only to be met by gunfire. In other parts of the city, white mobs began to lynch African Americans against the backdrop of burning buildings. As darkness came and the National Guard arrived, the violence began to wane but did not come to a complete stop. My grandparents barely escaped death with their young family and crossed the Mississippi River into safety in St. Louis, Missouri.

In response to the rioting, the National Association for the Advancement of Colored People (NAACP) sent Dr. W. E. B. Du Bois and Martha Gruening to investigate the incident. They compiled a report entitled "Massacre at East St. Louis," which was published in the NAACP's magazine, *The Crisis*. The NAACP also staged a silent protest march in New York City in response to the violence. Thousands of well-dressed African Americans marched down Fifth Avenue, showing their concern about the events in East St. Louis.

During World War II and after my grandfather's death, Hattie Ann Britton Duvall encouraged all five of her sons to enlist in the war. They enlisted in all the military branches during the war and were stationed in various parts of the world. My grandmother went to a department store in downtown St. Louis to shop and decided to go knowingly to a "white only" restaurant in the department store to get a cup of coffee. Challenging the segregation laws of the time, she sat down, and the waitress refused to serve her. Frustrated and yet resolute, she went home, made a sign, and came back to start a one-woman protest outside of the department store. Her sign read, "I gave my five sons to the war to defend this country, and I can't get a cup of coffee!" While her defiance and protesting certainly did not change segregation, I am sure that my grandmother felt satisfied that she confronted the unjust and racist laws of the Jim Crow era on that particular day. I now have immense esteem and honor for this blind yet heroic woman of God I called "Nanny." I now miss her imposing and sacred touch.

African American churches have long argued for a single creation of humans by God, consistent with the image of God. Biblical admonition asserts that creation was made in the image and likeness of God. Christians reference this as *imago Dei*: God created humans in God's image; therefore all humans are of the same substance and have the same relationship to God. Based on this, there can be no inferior or superior human beings. African-based traditions typically argue for the integrity of humans from the point of creation as well. In all these cases, there is nothing about the creation of humans or the look of any particular group of humans suggesting a divine strain of inferiority. Some within churches made an effort to attack directly the reading of Scripture used to justify slavery. They argued that the story of Ham does not promote the inferiority of Africans because it is not Ham who is cursed, but Canaan, Ham's son. And in response to the traditional interpretation of this Scripture, critics question the idea that God would obey the whims of a drunken man. Furthermore, some argue that the Christ event of the New Testament supersedes Hebrew Bible moral and ethical arrangements, and Christ makes no distinction between groups of humans. It is not that these various traditions do not acknowledge the difference in the physical look of different groups of humans. They do; however, they see these differences as having no impact on the beauty or importance of a given group, and they certainly do not see racial difference as justification for maltreatment.

Further justification and validation of a black biblical hermeneutic is given by the African American theologian, James Cone, who is generally regarded as the "father of black theology":

> *The hermeneutical principle for an exegesis of the Scriptures is the revelation of God in Christ as the Liberator of the oppressed from social oppression and to political struggle, wherein the poor recognize that their fight against poverty and injustice is not only consistent with the gospel but is the gospel of Jesus Christ.* . . . Any starting point that ignores God in Christ as the Liberator of the oppressed or that makes salvation as liberation secondary is *ipso facto* invalid and thus heretical. The test of the validity of this starting point, although dialectically related to black cultural experience, is not found in the particularity of the oppressed culture alone. It is found in the One who freely granted us freedom when we were doomed to slavery. In God's revelation in Scripture we come to the recognition that the divine liberation of the oppressed is not determined by our perceptions but by the God of the Exodus, the prophets, and Jesus Christ who calls the oppressed into a liberated existence. Divine revelation *alone is* the test of the validity of this starting point.[1]

---

1. James H. Cone, *God of the Oppressed* (New York: Seabury Press, 1975), 81–82 (emphasis in the original).

Observing Cone's thoughts on a black biblical hermeneutic, one could argue that a biblical emphasis on the social and political character of God's revelation in history for the weak and the helpless has important implications not only for the spiritual life of the Christian but for the work of theology as well. Therefore, black spirituality is biblical in that it is a retelling of what God has done in the past, is doing in the present, and has promised for the future. Finally, black spirituality is biblical because it risks being prophetic by doing theology from the perspective of those who are helpless and voiceless in this society.

Until the recent events of police brutality and killings of unarmed black men, the symbolism of Confederate flags and the continued existence of Confederate war hero monuments, and the blatant hatred and disrespect shown to President Barack Obama, one would have expected American society to progress forward in genuine efforts toward racial understanding and racial reconciliation in the twenty-first century. It is naïve to believe that we live in a "post-racial" society. Race still matters because race continues to separate, divide, disenfranchise, and marginalize. If we take the time to look and be aware, we will see that certain forms of dehumanization still exist. Symbols of power and domination can be found in degenerative public policies, lack of city services, inadequate code enforcement, construction of concrete jungles, inferior schools, excessive unemployment, efforts to repeal the Affordable Healthcare Act (Obamacare), and the war of drugs and violence. These elements are designed to impose humiliation on, strike fear into, and control the populations who are on the margins. This sets an atmosphere for people to self-destruct. In the immortal words of Marvin Gaye, "it makes me wanna holler and throw up both my hands!"[2]

From my youth, I have had an inherent sense of what is just and unjust—what is right and what is wrong. While I can certainly attribute my social consciousness to my strong Christian/Catholic formation and my socially aware and activist familial indoctrination, I also contend that this innate need to confront and eradicate social ills, most especially racism, is deeply embedded in my DNA. I unabashedly submit that being an activist or one who works for justice is not only learned behavior, influenced by one's upbringing and environment, but also is unquestionably genetic. I believe my commitment to speaking truth to power, being a voice for the voiceless, and my advocacy for a more just and humane society is due in large part because of knowing and valuing my personal genealogy for justice. As I have researched my family history, I have found not only Nanny, but other valiant men and women who have stories of their insistence on fighting against the evils of slavery, defying insane and unjust laws, and working for civil rights. There is little wonder why I am who I am and have demonstrated a strong commitment to justice. In my fifty plus years, I have found myself marching outside of the South African embassy against apartheid; working on the executive committee of my local branch of the NAACP; founding a community and economic development corporation to ensure community services that provided affordable housing for home ownership, jobs and job training, and businesses in

---

2. Marvin Gaye, "Inner City Blues (Make Me Wanna Holler)," written by Marvin Gaye and James Nyx, *What's Going On*, Motown Tamla Records, 1971.

impoverished neighborhoods; participating in the historic "Million Man March"; boycotting racist businesses and institutions; challenging corrupt political structures; combatting police brutality and inequality among police rank and file; and providing academic and recreational resources for urban youth. I have an innate desire and passion to leave places and people better than I have found them. My grandmother did it in her time, my mother and father did it during their time, and I have no excuse whatsoever to avoid answering my call to work for justice now. And I am edified to know that my grandnephew, a student at Yale University, was front-and-center in the protest to have the Ivy League university hire a more diverse faculty. The protest resulted in Yale University putting forth fifty million dollars to hire faculty members of color. Nanny would be so proud of her great-great-grandson.

Dr. Martin Luther King Jr. spoke of the urgency of now. My prayer and spirituality is at the heart of my urgency to work for justice. There is no convenient time to advocate for justice and equality. There is no better time than the present. You don't negotiate or comprise with evil; you confront it and eradicate it. The urgency of now compels one to act and to react immediately when witnessing on news reports black bodies being riddled with bullets, black bodies being choked to the point that they cannot breath, black bodies that are detained for no justifiable reason, and verbally and physically abused and humiliated simply to make the point that their black bodies and their black souls mean nothing. In essence, to show through brute force and unmitigated violence that whites are superior and those of the African Diaspora are deemed inferior. It can be interpreted through this intentional violence against black people that their lives were unimportant, insignificant, just didn't matter. Thus came the clarion call and the emergence of the social media phenomenon and #blacklivesmatter movement.

In 1979, the U.S. Catholic Bishops issued a pastoral letter on racism entitled "Brothers and Sisters to Us." The Catholic Bishops of the United States said in part:

> Racism is a sin: a sin that divides the human family, blots out the image of God among specific members of that family, and violates the fundamental human dignity of those called to be children of the same Father. Racism is the sin that says some human beings are inherently superior and others essentially inferior because of races. It is the sin that makes racial characteristics the determining factor for the exercise of human rights. It mocks the words of Jesus: "Treat others the way you would have them treat you." Indeed, racism is more than a disregard for the words of Jesus; it is a denial of the truth of the dignity of each human being revealed by the mystery of the Incarnation.[3]

Racial justice is not just a "people of color" cause; it's an American cause. The Black Lives Matter movement initially emerged in response to the shooting death of teenager Trayvon Martin by George Zimmerman in Florida. However, the movement took on an even larger visibility when it began focusing on

---

3. United States Conference of Catholic Bishops, "Brothers and Sisters to Us: U.S. Catholic Bishops Pastoral Letter on Racism," Washington, DC, November 14, 1979, p. 3.

the white police officers that shot and killed unarmed black males in Ferguson, Missouri; Cleveland and Cincinnati, Ohio; North Charleston, South Carolina; and Charlotte, North Carolina; as well as black people who died while in police custody in Staten Island, New York; Baltimore, Maryland; and in a county jail in Texas. Those tragic deaths were compounded when nine black people including their pastor were brutally killed by a young white man while attending Bible study in their church in Charleston, South Carolina.

What is an authentically Christian response to the Black Lives Matter movement, mass incarceration, and abuse of police power and de facto segregation? To paraphrase Rev. Dr. Martin Luther King Jr., we cannot be silent about the issues that matter. Statements and vigils simply do not suffice. What is needed is a meaningful commitment of equality and inclusion in our economy, communities, and churches. Moral theologian Father Bryan N. Massingale contends that the Catholic Church in America prioritizes "race relations" over "racial justice." He said, "People of faith need to understand that 'black lives matter' *is* a faith issue, which is rooted in something as old as our belief in creation. That if God created all of God's children with inimitable dignity, then the church needs to be in the forefront of advancing human dignity, whenever that is threatened or whenever that is undermined."[4]

---

4. Bryan N. Massingale, interview with Jarvis DeBerry, columnist, *Times-Picayune Newspaper*, at the Black Lives Matter Symposium sponsored by the Institute for Black Catholic Studies at Xavier University of Louisiana in New Orleans, LA, November 6, 2015.

When people rebuff the purpose of the Black Lives Matter movement by insisting "all lives matters," they not only miss the point that all lives are not at risk but also further diminish the realities of racism and oppression in our country. The Black Lives Matter movement challenges traditional norms of social movements. It is decentralized and creative: it has no one single leader; it is innovative with new media, modernizes civil disobedience, and maintains political and social pressure in the streets and at the policy table simultaneously. The Black Lives Matter movement is a movement that shows no signs of fading because in 2015 police killed nearly 1,200 people. Young Black men are nine times more likely to be killed by police than other Americans, despite their demographic only comprising 2 percent of the population.

While visiting a slum in Rio de Janerio on July 30, 2013, during World Youth Day, Pope Francis proclaimed,

I would like to make an appeal to those in possession of greater resources, to public authorities, and to all people of good will who are working for social justice: Never tire of working for a more just world, marked by greater solidarity! No one can remain insensitive to the inequalities that persist in the world! Everybody, according to his or her particular opportunities and responsibilities, should be able to make a personal contribution to putting an end to so many social injustices. The culture of selfishness and individualism that often prevails in our society is not what builds up and leads to a more habitable world: It is the culture of solidarity that does so, seeing others not as rivals or statistics, but brothers and sisters.

Many will pretend racism is a mere misunderstanding, and that, if we can just "get along," there will be racial peace in America. There are those who seek premature paths to promoting peace among the races before committing themselves to the painful acknowledgement of systemic racism in our nation and Church and their unwillingness to take the sometimes long journey toward making the necessary social, economic, political, systematic, and institutional changes to true and lasting peace. But peace is not a polite conversation between the oppressor and the oppressed. Peace is dismantling the hierarchies of oppression. Peace is redistribution of the economic and social power. Peace does not come from seeking the lowest common denominator, but in seeking radical and universal principles that will be fair to all.

Is it possible to dismantle white privilege? Evil is always incapable of critiquing itself. Evil depends upon disguise and tries to look like virtue. We have to fully cooperate in God's constant work, spoken so clearly in Mary's prayer (Luke 1:52), which is always "bringing down the mighty from their thrones and exalting the lowly." Unfortunately, power never surrenders without a fight. This is why some find the Black Lives Matter movement uncomfortable: if one's entire life has been to live unquestioned in their position of power that was culturally given to them, but they think that they have earned it, there is almost no way they will give it up without suffering, humiliation, or defeat.

It is often said that a society should be judged by how it treats "the least of these." But the fabric of our collective destiny depends on our commitment to eradicate inequity and render inequality irrelevant. If democracy and freedom are inherent values, the current status quo of racism and injustice—which benefits some over others—must be banished.

Sacred memory and genetic composition are two undeniable precious gifts that God has given me. I have been privileged to have a *Sankofa* moment—to go back and fetch a memory of a woman anchored in the Divine and resolute in making equality a reality for those who would come after her. I am blessed to remember that I am the grandson of Hattie Ann Britton Duvall. History books will never hold her name, but I hold her deep in my mind and close to my heart. This unflinching, unmovable, and undeterred educator, wife, mother, grandmother, great-grandmother, and great-great-grandmother, whom I lovingly called "Nanny," lives on in her descendants and thus her quest for justice continues.

Epilogue:
Contemplation in Action

Therese Taylor-Stinson

It seems that some people who call themselves contemplatives have merely found a way to justify their own procrastination or to explain their introversion or to defend their unwillingness to change in the face of injustice, remaining silent when there is a need to speak. I have learned that our practice of contemplation requires integration into our callings and lifestyles. So that contemplation can be whole, it must consist of both inward solitude and reflection, and an outward response to the situations in which we find ourselves present and awake.

In a chapter entitled "Traditional Methods of Contemplation and Action" in the book *Contemplation and Action in World Religions,* Elémire Zolla writes:

Modern [hu]man[s] [are] constantly tempted to seek spiritual life in sheer method, or else in some kind of blind rapture ringing with spontaneity and rich in creativity. Contemplation needs both. Method in itself leads only to disputation and quarrels. On the other hand, inspiration in itself, without the help of method, will lead to vain strivings toward creativity for its own sake. . . .

Contemplation soars above the archetypes and from these back up to the point from which everything arises.

Action is linked to the Greek *agonia*, which led to "agony": action in itself is always a sacrifice. When we leave the paradise of contemplation and descend to the earth of action, everything, including mystical action, becomes sacrificial. But agonia signifies "struggle," "contest," as well as "anguish," and esoterically speaking, an unseen warfare. It may well be that the point of failure in contemporary civilization was precisely the failure to realize the necessity of constantly fighting against evil.[1]

There is an evil in U.S. society that we term "racism." Racism is grounded in white superiority and privilege. It manifests itself in every aspect of life, including economics, education, employment, housing, health, beauty, relationships, religion, and spirituality. Racism can be identified as the American shadow. That shadow is also cast across the African continent, and over Europe, Australia, South America, and Asia.

In contemplative circles within the United States, racism shows up in the exclusion of people of color from the resources for contemplative practice, in the absence of leaders of color in

---

1. Elémire Zolla, "Traditional Modes of Contemplation and Action," in *Contemplation and Action in World Religions: Selected Papers from the Rothko Chapel Colloquium,* ed. Yusuf Ibish and Ileana Marculescu (1977; Seattle: University of Washington Press, 1978), 105.

contemplative organizations and movements, in the absence of many people of color in most contemplative programs and conferences, and in the resistance to acknowledging this shortcoming and changing it. How can we, as contemplatives, turn away from the spiritual disease of racism, ignore the sacrificial, and fail to fight to eliminate the presence of racism from our own path, and then proclaim that we are to chart the path of contemplation in the spirit of tradition?

Jack Finley once said, "The mystic is known by the quality of their empathy, integrity, by the authenticity of your presence with each. You cannot express the beauty of yourself and hide at the same time."[2]

Do we justify the quality of our empathy and integrity, do we manifest an authentic presence ourselves when we turn a deaf ear and our backs to the ways we use our privilege and affluence to deny the presence of a people and their authentic presence and participation in a spiritual tradition, either consciously or unconsciously?

Contemplation calls for both practice and integration. We cannot claim contemplation as our authentic lifestyle if we fail to turn our practice into habits and our reflections into awareness and action.

Feminist and activist Audre Lorde wrote, "The transformation of silence into language and action is an act of self-revelation and that always seems fraught with danger. But my daughter . . . said, 'tell them about how you're never really a whole person if you

---

2. "Stories of Thomas Merton" with James Finley, presentation, Shalem Institute's annual Gerald May Seminar, Universalist Unitarian Congregation of Rockville, Maryland, April 24, 2015.

remain silent, because there's always that one little piece inside of you that wants to be spoken out.'"[3]

Our need to stay safe, to protect our socially constructed status in the world, is ego driven, and as much as we need our egos to maintain the status quo, to defend that which renders a whole group virtually invisible, unworthy of holding place in the world, is not an act of careful discernment, but an act of privilege and a false sense of superiority.

I must speak when injustice is revealed to me, and my speaking must be evidenced in my actions. Dr. Martin Luther King Jr. said, "There comes a time when silence is betrayal. . . . In the end, we will remember not the words of our enemies, but the silence of our friends."[4] To be authentic, contemplation must indwell action and all action must follow contemplation. There is where we live into the call of Jesus and carry on the authentic tradition of social activism in Christianity:

> "The Spirit of the Lord is upon me,
> because he has anointed me
> to bring good news to the poor.
> He has sent me to proclaim release to the captives
> and recovery of sight to the blind,
> to let the oppressed go free." (Luke 4:18)

---

3. Audre Lorde, "The Transformation of Silence into Language and Action," speech, Lesbian and Literature panel, Modern Language Association meeting, Chicago, Illinois, December 28, 1977.
4. Rev. Dr. Martin Luther King Jr., "Beyond Vietnam: A Time to Break Silence," speech, meeting of Clergy and Laity Concerned, Riverside Church, New York City, April 4, 1967.

As Christians, we are called to full communion with the Christ-spirit—a spirit of witness and sacrifice, "martyria," which means to be one who is willing to suffer for what has been seen and heard. Not only Christians, but the whole created order! As living beings, we are called to authentic contemplation, which begins with method that leads into sacrificial action to support the balance of life. Therefore, we cannot proclaim that all lives matter until we have born witness to the lives of those who have been treated less than our own. We must first acknowledge that not only all lives matter, LBGT lives matter, female lives matter, children's lives matter, and yes, Black lives matter in all of their resplendent hues and cultures. We must bear witness to their gifts, their contributions to life as we know it, and to their very foundational influence to that which we call contemplation.

Racism is a deeply imbedded and dark spiritual disease that must be brought to the light and exposed for how it has inhibited the balance of life. It starts, I think, with those who believe they are enlightened and carry tools for discernment and healing in a broken world.

About the Authors

Reverend Ineda P. Adesanya, MA, MDiv, DASD, is an ordained American Baptist minister and spiritual director. She received both her master of divinity with concentration in Christian Spirituality and her diploma in the Art of Spiritual Direction from the San Francisco Theological Seminary. Ineda serves as the Minister of Spiritual Life for Allen Temple Baptist Church in Oakland, California, and authors a weekly blog entitled "Spiritual Life Note" for the congregation and community. Ineda is founder and proprietor of *WJoy—A Spiritual Care Ministry* serving faith-based institutions, clergy, and lay members of the community.

Lerita Coleman Brown, PhD, is a spiritual director/companion, writer, speaker, workshop leader, and professor of psychology emerita at Agnes Scott College in Decatur, Georgia. Lerita writes about and promotes the life and work of Howard Thurman, contemplative spirituality, and uncovering the peace and joy in one's heart on her website peaceforhearts.com, Facebook peaceforhearts, and on Twitter @peace4hearts.

Vikki Montgomery is a contemplative, communications consultant, writer, and educator. She has served as a pilgrimage leader and companion at the Center for Prayer and Pilgrimage at the Washington National Cathedral for several years. She earned an MTS and MA in theology from Wesley Theological Seminary. In 2015, she was received as an associate of the Holy Cross, an Episcopal monastery in New York.

Ruqaiyah Nabe, RN, DMin, is an interfaith minister and spiritual director serving the Muslim and interspiritual communities. As an independent practitioner, she officiates at rites and rituals of life-cycle events. She also responds to requests for speaking engagements and interfaith dialogue. She's a graduate of the One Spirit Interfaith Seminary's ministry and interspiritual counseling programs, and she earned her doctor of ministry degree from New York Theological Seminary. She may be contacted at ruqaiyahn@gmail.com.

Rev. Rosalie Norman-McNaney is an ordained American Baptist minister, spiritual director, and hospice chaplain in Central Florida. Norman-McNaney is committed to sharing the transformational love of the gospel of Jesus Christ in ministry with all people regardless of race, culture, ethnicity, language, age, sexual orientation, and ability.

Maurice J. Nutt, CSsR, DMin, is director of the Institute for Black Catholic Studies at Xavier University, New Orleans, Louisiana. A spiritual director since 1994, Father Nutt was a member of the Redemptorist Parish Mission Preaching Team in Chicago, Illinois. He is the author of *Thea Bowman: In My Own Words; Advent and Christmas Wisdom from St. Alphonsus Liguori;* and *Lent and Easter Wisdom from St. Alphonsus Liguori.* He is also a contributor to the *African American Catholic Youth Bible,* a collaborative project between the National Black Catholic Congress and St. Mary's Press, published in 2013, and *Embodied Spirits: Stories of Spiritual Directors of Color* (Morehouse Publishing, 2014).

Jung Eun Sophia Park, SNJM, PhD, is an assistant professor in religious studies at the Holy Names University, and also practices spiritual direction in the San Francisco Bay Area, California. Park is the author of *A Hermeneutic on Dislocation as Experience: Creating a Borderland Constructing a Hybrid Identity* (Peter Lang, 2009), and she has published numerous articles on spirituality and spiritual direction in particular, including "Cross Cultural Spiritual Direction: Dance with a Stranger," "When One Feels Caught in a Pattern," and "Religious Life in the US: A Vocation of Border Crossing." Her research focuses on cross-cultural spiritual direction from a global perspective.

Soyinka Rahim, Grassroots Spiritual Practitioner (GSP), was born and raised in Oakland, California. She is a teacher, artist, singer, dancer, writer, poet, Interplay facilitator, spiritual director, and an activist for BIBOLOVE—Breathe in! Breathe out! Love! BIBO (breathe in, breathe out, with a focused breath—roar, sigh, hum, yum, shhh). Facebook: Soyinka Rahim; website: http://www .soyinkarahim.com

Gigi Ross lives in Albuquerque, New Mexico, where she works as administrative coordinator for education at the Center for Action and Contemplation. She practices spiritual direction and sings with the Albuquerque chapter of the Threshold Choir, which ministers in song to those who are dying.

Rabbi Leslie Schotz is an ordained spiritual director with a doctorate in ministry. The title of her dissertation and first book is *Spiritual Direction for Jewish Children*. Her second book is *Shalom: A Congregational Guide to Jewish Meditation*.

Jacquelyn Smith-Crooks, EdD, former director of Community Outreach Programs at Harvard Medical School and founding executive director of Macedonia Church Family Life Center, is a life coach and spiritual director. She works with people on issues of change and transformation in leadership and organizations. Jacquelyn works with people individually and in groups, as well as leads retreats, workshops, and presents keynote speeches at meetings. She currently resides in Amherst, Massachusetts, and is available for sessions in person or by other media means.

Maisie Sparks received her certification in the art of spiritual direction from the Christos Center for Spiritual Formation in Lino Lake, Minnesota. She offers contemplative retreats and workshops for women, sharing the difference between being still and doing nothing. A freelance writer, Maisie is the author of *Holy Shakespeare!*, *Christmas Quiet*, *151 Things God Can't Do*, and other titles.

Therese Taylor-Stinson is a graduate of the Shalem Institute for Spiritual Formation, where she is also a member of the Shalem Society for Contemplative Leadership. Therese has maintained a private spiritual direction practice for more than twelve years. She is an ordained deacon and elder in the Presbyterian Church (USA), and a certified lay pastoral caregiver. Therese, a retired federal employee, is a founder and the managing member of the

Spiritual Directors of Color Network, Ltd., and a contributing author and coeditor of *Embodied Spirits: Stories of Spiritual Directors of Color*. You can reach her at taylorstinson@earthlink.com; Twitter: SpiritWings11; as well as on Facebook.